AF437732

REPEATABLE

How to Build A Home Service Business that Grows Itself

SHARON TINBERG MINGEY

REPEATABLE

Copyright © 2026 by Sharon Tinberg Mingey.

MILTON & HUGO L.L.C.
1001 3rd Avenue West, Suite 430
Bradenton, FL 34205, USA

Website: *www. miltonandhugo.com*
Hotline: *1- 888-778-0033*
Email: *info@miltonandhugo.com*

Ordering Information:
Quantity sales. Special discounts are granted to corporations, associations, and other organizations. For more information on these discounts, please reach out to the publisher using the contact information provided above.

Library of Congress Control Number: 2026906633
ISBN-13: 979-8-89285-827-4 [Paperback Edition]
979-8-89285-828-1 [Hardback Edition]
979-8-89285-829-8 [Digital Edition]

Rev. date: 03/10/2026

CONTENTS

Acknowledgment vii

Introduction xi

Chapter 1   The Owner's Odyssey 1

Chapter 2   Navigating Survival Mode 5

Chapter 3   Leveraging the Big Breaks 11

Chapter 4   Building Bridges and Relationships 21

Chapter 5   Leveraging Free Television Advertising ...34

Chapter 6   The Cost of Stability 44

Chapter 7   Growth Requires Employees 55

Chapter 8   Meticulously Managing the Details 76

Chapter 9   The Cost of Not Training Well 82

Chapter 10   Training Before the First House 90

Chapter 11   The Unforeseen Truth 101

Chapter 12   Managing Team Players 115

Chapter 13   Growing a Team That Wants to Stay ...129

Chapter 14   The Great Scam 135

Chapter 15   Beware of Attorneys 143

Chapter 16   The Software Saga 154

Chapter 17   The Discipline of Choice 165

Chapter 18   Putting Hope Where Others Think
                There Is None 170

Chapter 19   Leadership vs. Management: Where
                Leadership Actually Happens 176

Chapter 20   Anchored in the Wrong Port 183

Chapter 21   Where the Real Lessons Live 187

Final Words...193

ACKNOWLEDGMENT

In a world that is changing faster than ever, where it's easy to feel ungrounded and pulled in a dozen directions at once, there is my book, *Repeatable: How to Build a Service Business that Grows Itself.* More than just a book, it is a testament to the power of steady effort, lessons learned through repeated hard work, consistent grace, ongoing resilience, and the unwavering support of extraordinary people who stood beside me repeatedly. As I move through the chapters of life's business, I find comfort in dedicating these words to those who shaped my journey not just once, but through years of shared experience and steadfast presence.

To my incredible mother, Evelyn Tinberg, a beacon of love and grace, who taught me that the smallest acts, done faithfully over time, shape a life. She showed me that love is not just spoken; it is demonstrated repeatedly in daily sacrifice, steady kindness, and quiet strength. Through her example, I learned that compassion is not an event, but a pattern, and that true grace is built through consistent care.

To my liberal and inspiring father, Wallace Tinberg, whose belief in my abilities was not a single moment of encouragement but a steady drumbeat throughout my life. His message was simple: Enduring hard work, repeated faithfully, opens doors that talent alone cannot. His resilience, shown day after day, and his constant support gave me the confidence to keep moving forward, especially when progress felt slow. He taught me that success is rarely sudden; it is earned through steady steps.

A heartfelt nod to my steadfast friends Sharon Fliess, Bonnie Schmidt and Greg, Chris and Lisa (Haughney) Prey, whose support didn't just appear in the big moments but showed up consistently through the years. Through triumphs and tribulations, they stood by me, offering encouragement, perspective, and understanding whenever I needed it. Their friendship has been a reliable anchor, proof that support, like success, is built through showing up repeatedly.

To my sister, Shelby Schirz, a dependable presence in every season of life. Her support has never been loud, but it has been constant. She reminds me that we are never truly alone when we have someone who continues to stand beside us, year after year. The strength of our bond is not found in grand gestures but in shared history, repeated understanding, and quiet loyalty.

To my industry family, the Blaze Brigade: Jeff Marquie, Mario George, Marlo Kanipe, Adriana Olivares, and Kristina LaVerne. For nearly two decades, you have been my colleagues, my clients, and my friends. We didn't just work together; we grew together—one project, one challenge, one improvement at a time. Your honesty, encouragement, and advocacy have shaped not only this work, but the path that made it possible.

And to Rich Reese, for standing with me from the start; Josh Brown, for pushing me to finish what I began; and Paul Freed, for championing my mission and helping bring this book to life.

To Keri Woehl, my steadfast business support partner for thirty-six remarkable years. Without Keri, there would be no story of The Upstairs Maid to tell. Hiring Keri at just eighteen and a half years old was the best decision I ever made. Her dedication wasn't just a burst of effort; it was a pattern. Night after night, year after year, she showed up, often circling back to the office after hours to keep things moving forward. Her commitment turned daily effort into long-term progress, and her consistency helped transform a small business into something real and lasting. Keri didn't just work hard; she worked faithfully—and that made all the difference.

Last but certainly not least, a profound acknowledgment to my husband, Jim Mingey, whose presence in my life has been a steady force for growth and change. His impact wasn't found in one dramatic moment, but in the way his influence gradually shifted the trajectory of my life. Sometimes transformation doesn't happen in a single decision; it happens through consistent encouragement, steady belief, and shared vision.

As you read *Repeatable*, you may see that success is rarely built in dramatic leaps, but through steady patterns of action, support, and learning. This book is more than ink on paper; it is the story of how repeated effort, repeated lessons, and repeated support shape a life. Together, let us move through these pages with the understanding that progress comes not from trying once, but from continuing forward, again and again.

INTRODUCTION

Over the course of my life, I've come to understand that the difference of a wildly successful life, an average one, or even failure, rarely comes down to talent, luck, or opportunity. It comes down to the ability to do the right things over and over again, and to keep improving them. Success is not built on bursts of motivation; it is built on repeatable discipline. The people who build strong businesses and meaningful lives aren't the ones who rise to the occasion once in a while. They are the ones who commit to steady action, refine their habits, and stay with something long enough to see the compound results.

Activity matters, but activity alone is not the answer. Plenty of people stay busy and still go nowhere. Real progress comes from focused, repeatable effort, doing what works, adjusting it, and doing it again tomorrow. That kind of steady execution may not look dramatic; but it is the quiet force behind every stable business, every lasting career, and every life that moves forward instead of sideways.

I learned this lesson long before I owned a business. I learned it growing up on a Wisconsin dairy farm where consistency wasn't optional and discipline came before comfort. The cows had to be milked twice a day, every day, no exceptions for Saturdays, Sundays, holidays, illness, or "a bad day." The work didn't depend on how we felt. It depended on repetition.

Farmers in those days couldn't afford to waste effort or have inconsistent habits. Their lives were built on routines that had to be repeated faithfully: feeding animals, fixing equipment, tending fields, caring for family. Their love, their faith, and their commitment to daily responsibility formed a steady foundation. They didn't talk about discipline; they lived it.

My childhood on that farm was marked by simplicity and love. My mother's devotion wasn't occasional; it was constant. Staying up late to sew our clothes, cooking meals from scratch, caring for the home, she showed me that love is built through repeated acts of care. Her work wasn't glamorous, but it was consistent, and that consistency shaped us more than any one grand gesture ever could.

My parents didn't just teach me values; they modeled repeatable behavior. If something needed to be done, it got done, properly and consistently. That principle became the foundation of everything I would later build, and it is the heart of this book: Success comes from doing the right things often enough and long enough for the results to multiply.

Setting priorities is the linchpin of success; and it's often the small decisions, repeated daily, that determine whether a business grows or struggles. When faced with choosing between a million-dollar meeting and delivering a feather duster to a cleaner, which task truly moves the business forward? This book explores how consistent priorities and repeatable systems, not occasional heroic effort, create lasting success.

As I pen these words, I find myself reflecting on the remarkable journey that has shaped my life. For the first two decades, my path was carefully influenced and guided by my father. His direction wasn't loud or forceful, but steady and consistent. He believed in structure, in responsibility, and in doing things the right way repeatedly until they became second nature. That early guidance formed patterns in me long before I understood how valuable those patterns would become.

Growing up on a farm in the 1950s, I knew farming wasn't glamorous. It was a simple life, and we didn't even have running water until I was six years old. As farm kids, we often felt different at school, like we came from another world. We were the true meaning of "country when country wasn't cool." But what felt ordinary to us then was actually an education in repetition, responsibility, and resilience.

Television wasn't part of my early childhood. My world was shaped by books, school, radio, and, most importantly, my parents. They didn't just tell me how to live, they showed me, day after day. My father's words still echo in my mind: "It's not what you do, but how you do it. Strive for excellence, and success will be your companion." What he really meant was this: Do things well, do them consistently, and keep improving. That mindset later gave me the confidence to pursue a career in telemarketing when it was still called phone sales. Even when my father initially questioned that path, the values he had repeated into me allowed me to rise through the ranks, eventually managing over a thousand salespeople.

Years later, when my parents visited my office on the thirteenth floor overlooking the Capitol building in Austin, my father beamed with pride. When someone asked how I was doing, he proudly shared that I was managing a telemarketing team of over a thousand people. What stayed with me wasn't just his pride, but the realization that the work itself hadn't changed, only the label had. What was once "phone sales" had become "telemarketing," and suddenly, it sounded respectable. That moment reinforced a lesson I would see repeatedly in business: Perception may shift, but consistent performance is what truly builds success.

That realization gave me the courage to walk away from a comfortable $80,000 management position in 1988 to start a home-service business. It wasn't an impulsive decision. It was another step built on the same repeatable habits I had practiced my whole life: Show up, do the work, improve the process, and keep going. That decision, and the systems it forced me to create, became the foundation for everything in this book.

My parents didn't just teach me the value of excellence; they taught me that how you do something matters more than what you accomplish. *Integrity* wasn't a word we used on the farm; it was simply how we lived. You didn't cut corners on milking because the cows depended on consistency. If my dad skipped a milking, no neighbor might know, but the cows would. Miss one milking and the cow would begin the drying-up cycle. They would still produce milk, just not as much. Miss repeatedly, and production would steadily drop. The outcome was directly tied to repeated action.

The same was true for pulling weeds. If I skipped rows, my father might not notice right away, but the field would show it soon enough. The work had to be done right, not because someone was watching but because results come from repeating the right actions every single time.

Years later, I saw that same truth play out in the cleaning business. If you miss a cleaning one time and must reschedule, most clients will understand. Life happens. But trust drops just a tiny bit. Do it again, and it drops a little more. Overtime, reliability, or the lack of it, becomes part of how the client sees your company. The same goes for the small details. Leave one light switch plate uncleaned and the client probably won't notice. Leave it untouched for six or eight visits, and that frequently used switch will become visibly dirty. That's when the client starts wondering what else is being missed. Trust doesn't disappear all at once. It erodes through repeated neglect, just as it grows through repeated care.

That lesson became the foundation of everything I built. Integrity isn't something you add to a business after it becomes successful; it's what you build the business on. Every system I created, every employee I trained, every client I served, and every difficult decision I made came back to one question: Is this the right thing to do? Not the easy thing. Not the fast thing. The right thing. Because over time, doing the right thing consistently builds trust, and trust is one of the most valuable assets any business can have.

Clients trust you. Employees respect you. And when challenges come, and they always do, you can sleep at night knowing you did what you said you would do, the way you said you would do it. That peace of mind isn't built in one big decision; it's built through thousands of small, repeatable choices.

Over time, what started as my own survival story turned into something bigger. After I built The Upstairs Maid into a real company, with systems, standards, and repeatable results, other owners began asking me how I did it. One request turned into another, and before I knew it, I was consulting with home-service owners and helping them build what we had built: training that worked, structure that reduced chaos, and leadership that kept people. Most of the stories in this book come from my years inside my own company. Some come from offices and field training days with owners I coached, because watching other businesses succeed, or struggle, taught me just as much as building my own.

With great pleasure and a deep sense of purpose, I present to you my inaugural book, *Repeatable: How to Build a Service Business that Grows Itself.* I extend my sincere gratitude to you for choosing it and trusting me with your time. My hope is that within these pages, you will discover not just inspiration, but practical lessons you can repeat in your own business, actions you can apply again and again until they create lasting success of your own.

CHAPTER 1

THE OWNER'S ODYSSEY

The calendar marked the dawning of a new week, one that would etch into my memory as the onset of an extraordinary journey. It was the year 1988, and I had just taken the bold step of resigning from my managerial position at MCI Long Distance company. This pivotal decision marked my transition into the role of co-owner of The Upstairs Maid.

As I embarked on this new path, I was met with an intriguing question: What exactly does a co-owner do on their inaugural day of this unique journey? To complicate matters further, there were no well-defined "owner" job descriptions to follow, a reality that is not true today for independent owners. In this pre-Internet era, my resources were limited, with only three rolodex cards at the library dedicated to residential cleaning services, an unlikely starting point, but one I eagerly explored. In my quest for knowledge, I stumbled upon the wisdom of Jeff Campbell, encapsulated within three modest paperbacks. I wasted no time in procuring each of them.

The initial week of my ownership was unconventional, to say the least. Instead of launching into the operational intricacies of our fledgling business, I undertook a task that many new owners might never contemplate: I set about writing a comprehensive employee handbook. It was an endeavor that would yield remarkable dividends in the years to come.

Among the valuable assets I carried with me from my previous role at MCI Long Distance was a 350-page employee handbook. With painstaking dedication, I meticulously condensed it into a concise thirty-two-page document. Within the span of that first week, I single-handedly crafted the mission, values, policies, and regulations that would serve as the bedrock upon which The Upstairs Maid would evolve into a multimillion-dollar enterprise.

However, this transformative initiative did not sit well with the five existing part-time employees who had been managing the company alongside my husband, Mike, the owner of The Upstairs Maid, for the past year. It's important to note that neither Mike nor I started The Upstairs Maid from scratch, which conferred upon us a significant advantage in our rapid ascent. As with many success stories, we were blessed with a few strokes of luck. Acquiring thirty repeat clients for $30,000 in 1986 might have seemed a bit expensive, but it was actually a fortuitous break that provided us with a vital head start. Securing the first one hundred clients can be an arduous undertaking, and having this initial foundation significantly eased our uphill climb. The acquisition of an existing company expedited this process, delivering one hundred repeat clients to our doorstep in just ninety days.

Climbing from thirty to ninety repeat clients in such a short period without the Internet was due to an even more significant windfall, a treasure trove of files belonging to canceled clients. In 1980, eight years before we purchased it, The Upstairs Maid boasted an impressive roster of ninety-four repeat clients, an achievement made remarkable by the era's prevailing norms. In those times, it was virtually unheard of to allow strangers into one's home without the homeowner's vigilant presence, especially in the state of Texas. The Upstairs Maid had meticulously carved its name into the community's consciousness and even graced the front page of the esteemed *Austin American Statesman*. This feature substantially boosted the original owner's income and introduced newfound wealth into their lives. Unfortunately, alongside this prosperity came the pitfalls of excess, leading to the misuse of newfound resources in the form of alcohol and cocaine. Within seven years, this mismanagement nearly plunged the company into bankruptcy, leaving behind only thirty loyal clients and a trail of negative publicity. Had the Internet and Google reviews existed, the remnants of the company would have surely withered away.

At that juncture, our mortgage was anchored to my corporate salary, a monthly obligation of $799 at a rather imposing 9 percent interest rate. We had no supplementary income sources; and this situation, perhaps paradoxically, turned out to be a blessing in disguise. Our fledgling cleaning company had no choice but to succeed. With modest savings of around $125,000, I held on to it with an almost irrational caution, wary of the uncertainties that accompanied this newfound venture.

My role within our nascent home-service company encompassed sales and customer service, while I also assumed the responsibilities of staff recruitment, management, billing, and virtually every aspect except the actual cleaning of homes. In contrast, Mike's responsibilities, my husband and sole business partner, centered on window cleaning and carpet steam cleaning. In those early days, I was the sole office presence, wearing multiple hats that spanned administration, operations, management, and sales.

Having dedicated that initial week to crafting the employee handbook, I found myself at an impasse yet again, with the realization that we urgently needed to grow our client base. With only thirty recurring clients, our income wouldn't be enough to cover our expenses. We needed new business, and we needed it fast. But I also understood something that would shape every decision from that point forward: Not all sales are created equal. One-time jobs bring activity. Repeat clients build businesses.

I had always worked with goals. In my corporate career, they were tied to budgets and monthly performance targets. In my personal life, I set annual goals to keep myself moving forward. Now I applied the same discipline here. I knew exactly how many repeat clients we had and how much each one was worth on average. Starting with those thirty recurring customers was an enormous advantage because it allowed me to see, from the very beginning, the true value of repeat clients. I calculated how much revenue we needed to survive, then projected what it would take to reach one million dollars in annual gross revenue. I had no idea whether that goal was realistic, but when I broke it down, it came to something surprisingly simple: one new repeat client per week for ten years at current prices.

Of course, I also knew from my sales background that cancellations would chip away at our progress. So I created a tracking system the only way I knew how: visually and publicly. On the back of a roll of extra wallpaper I had lying around, I built a wall chart with columns for working days, new repeat clients, cancellations, net gain, goal, and plus or minus against that goal. Revenue was the math behind the plan, but repeat clients were the driver. Some type of wall chart hung on some wall in every office I ever had. It guided every sales effort, every networking conversation, and every growth decision. That's why I can tell you, decades later, that I left the business with 754 repeat clients. Most owners can tell you their monthly revenue. Very few can tell you exactly how many repeat clients they have. And that, I've come to believe, is at the heart of why running a home-service business feels so hard for so many owners: They are chasing sales instead of building a repeatable base.

CHAPTER 2

NAVIGATING SURVIVAL MODE

There's a certain allure to being an owner, one that demands versatility and adaptability. In my case, I was a jack-of-all-trades, a multifaceted individual with a portfolio of skills and experiences. Oddly enough, this diverse skill set proved immensely beneficial as I embarked on the journey of establishing a new business. Prior to securing the position at MCI, I had navigated through an array of sixteen different jobs in just twelve years, savoring the eclectic taste of various roles. From sales representative and bookkeeper to bill collector and telemarketing manager, I had donned numerous hats on my journey. My career had taken me from being a district phone sales trainer to eventually managing MCI's one thousand sales representatives. In the backdrop of the corporate world, it was often advised for women in their twenties to switch jobs every two years. While I shrank that timeframe to a mere eight months, each transition brought me increased compensation, loftier titles, and larger organizations with deeper pockets. It was this trajectory that had culminated in my securing such a large salary in 1986.

Now, as a co-owner of my own enterprise, I am presented with an opportunity to amalgamate the talents instilled by my mother during my formative years on the farm and the wealth of work and management experience I had amassed in both the private and corporate sectors.

In the relentless pursuit of more clients, I turned my attention to the boxes filled with records of canceled clients that had come with the acquisition of the business. For ninety consecutive days, I embarked on a nightly ritual of dialing the phone one hundred times. This may have seemed like a daunting task, but my previous role as the telemarketing manager for one thousand employees at MCI Long Distance had equipped me with the knowledge to tackle it effectively. Though I wasn't particularly fond of this task, it was a necessary step. Our savings account was dwindling rapidly, and we found ourselves at a pivotal crossroads. We needed an infusion of funds to sustain our venture. Returning to the corporate world was not an option I relished, making telemarketing a more favorable alternative. It wasn't just about trying to find more money; it was a matter of survival.

Numbers and statistics were my compass through this ordeal. I believed that by dialing the phone one hundred times each night, I would secure an average of one sale per day, if not more. To keep track, I diligently marked each set of four calls on a blank sheet of paper, with a fifth diagonal line crossing every fourth line. After the calls, I didn't just set the phone down and call it a night. I would walk straight over to the wall chart I had made and record what happened that day: sales, cancellations, net gain, and whether I was ahead or behind my goal. I was meticulous about it. I'd stand there with my pen, almost holding my breath, hoping I could check off that I had hit the number I needed. Some nights it felt like a win. Other nights, especially when a cancellation came in, it felt like the air went out of the room. But that chart did something important for me: It kept me focused on the only thing that mattered—building a repeatable base. I wasn't chasing activity. I was building stability, one repeat client at a time.

As my reward for this relentless endeavor, I would enjoy a humble glass of boxed wine while joining Mike for a simple hot dog. My telemarketing efforts extended to approximately 2.5 hours of calls each evening, supplemented by a productive Saturday morning session. Saturday mornings proved to be particularly fruitful. My usual calling hours were from 6:30 p.m. to 9:00 p.m., four nights a week, and Saturdays from 9:00 a.m. to 1:00 p.m. In our modest 1,300-square-foot home, I occupied the back bedroom while Mike watched TV and savored his hotdogs. Strangely, we hadn't cashed any of the paychecks we earned since leaving my MCI job. They were merely issued to ensure we met our tax obligations weekly. Those were undoubtedly challenging times, yet as I reflect upon them, they were profoundly fulfilling. Crafting business goals and witnessing our enterprise achieve them made me a firm believer in the power of statistics, numbers, and, most importantly, in myself.

Telemarketing a service or product often falls under the category of endeavors one succeeds at because no one else is willing to do it. There were nights when I found myself fervently praying that no one would answer the phone, as I lacked the inclination to engage in conversations. However, I knew that dialing the phone one hundred times each night would yield an average of one sale per night, so regardless of how I felt, I kept on dialing for dollars/ clients.

My approach to prospects was candid and distinctive. I picked up the phone, took a deep breath, and launched into my pitch.

"Hello, this is Sharon Butza with The Upstairs Maid. We've recently acquired the company and brought it under new management. Our approach is rooted in value and processes."

There would usually be a pause on the other end. These words were a novelty in the realm of home-service businesses back in 1986.

"I'm calling because I noticed you were a client a few years ago," I continued. "May I ask, have you found another cleaning service?"

Most hadn't. Some had tried one or two others and given up entirely.

"Would you consider giving us another chance? We're not the same company you remember. We won't charge you an additional first-time initial fee, just our regular rate."

Some people said yes immediately. Others needed more convincing. A few had already switched to services they were satisfied with, and I didn't attempt to sway them away. For those, I simply said, "I completely understand. I'm going to send you a note with our business card anyway. If anything changes, we'd love to hear from you."

Although I had hoped for more than thirty sales, the endeavor proved well worth the time and incurred no additional cost, effectively doubling our income.

Our momentum was palpable, but a new challenge loomed on the horizon: We were running out of prospects to call. It's important to note that during this period, we felt our financial constraints were too substantial to allocate funds toward traditional advertising methods such as Yellow Pages, newspapers, magazines, or radio, not to mention the expenses of hiring professionals to create advertisements. In those days, personal computers with the capability to craft flyers or digital marketing materials were a futuristic concept. Determined to press on, I resorted to unconventional measures.

I crafted flyers using carbon paper and a coloring book. My strategy was to distribute these flyers on the homes situated on hills in Austin, specifically targeting those with houses on only one side of the street. I surmised that no one else would be enthusiastic or perhaps daring enough to venture into such an endeavor. While ascending the hills and placing flyers on the homes, I would daydream about homeowners becoming repeat clients. Regrettably, the journey downhill proved futile, as there were no homes to target with flyers. However, while heading uphill, I seized the unique opportunity to be the sole flyer on the door, effectively doubling my outreach efforts.

The next step in my quest was to procure a tool known as a Crisscross Directory. This invaluable resource provided me with addresses corresponding to the homes where I had placed flyers, along with the phone numbers of the residents. It was an efficient method that I wish were still available today. In our current era, characterized by cell phones and a scarcity of landlines, such directories have become a rarity.

I dialed the number of every home I had visited.

Ring, ring, ring.

"Hello?"

"Hi, this is Sharon with The Upstairs Maid. I left a flyer on your door yesterday about our cleaning services. Did you happen to see it?"

"Oh yes, I did see that."

"Wonderful. I just wanted to follow up personally and see if you had any questions about our services. We specialize in repeat cleanings and offer very competitive rates."

Most of them responded positively to my calls, and this concerted effort led to another thirty sales within a span of two months. Word of mouth began to gain momentum, and we secured ten referral sales in those ninety days, ultimately achieving our goal of reaching one hundred repeat clients within ninety days. Fortunately, I never had to make another telemarketing call myself, for which I was immensely grateful. From that point forward, there was no looking back.

At the time, I didn't realize just how much that experience would shape my understanding of growth. I thought I was simply doing what needed to be done to survive. It never occurred to me that this focus on rebuilding relationships and creating repeat clients was unusual. I assumed every service business owner understood that stability comes from returning to people who already know and trust you.

Years later, after consulting with cleaning companies all over the country, some doing one million, some doing five million, I realized something that still shocks me. Many of these businesses are sitting on gold mines they don't even recognize. They have lists of past one-time customers and canceled repeat clients—five thousand names, ten thousand names, sometimes fifteen thousand names, people who already trusted them once, people whose information they already paid to acquire. And those names just sit there. Untouched.

Instead, they spend thousands of dollars every month, some every week, buying new leads and training sales reps to "close better" or to "convert one-times into repeats." But here's what I've seen repeatedly: If someone wants recurring service, they usually buy recurring service. If they want a one-time clean, that's what they're shopping for. You can improve scripts and follow-up all day long, but you can't force a one-time buyer to suddenly want an ongoing commitment.

The simplest, most profitable move is the one most owners ignore: Go back and recapture what you already earned. Call the canceled repeats. Reintroduce yourself. Fix what broke. And for the one-time customers? At least check back in. Many companies don't even ask if they need another cleaning. That's wasted opportunity and wasted money. I worked hard with a few hundred names to build a base of repeat clients. Today, businesses are sitting on thousands of names and acting like they have nothing to work with, so they keep chasing new sales like an ambulance, instead of building something repeatable. Sometimes I look at those untouched lists and think, *I'd love to open an office in their city and work those leads myself. I could probably match their revenue in two years just by doing what they're not doing.*

CHAPTER 3

LEVERAGING THE BIG BREAKS

My next significant breakthrough occurred when the chamber of commerce sought an expert to teach telemarketing skills to its members. Ironically, although phone sales had been practiced since the 1970s, telemarketing was still relatively novel. Despite its apparent simplicity, few people truly understood how to make those calls effectively. To be frank, I'm not entirely convinced that anyone truly understands how to use the phone for sales even today. Back then, Austin, in particular, recognized the power of this cost-effective marketing tool due to the influx of telemarketing centers. My experience helping establish MCI Long Distance company's telemarketing center in Austin during my transition from Dallas added to my credentials. Simultaneously, Michael Dell was emerging as a self-made multimillionaire through his telemarketing centers selling computers in Austin. The city, with its university brimming with students seeking part-time work, had transformed into a burgeoning tech hub.

The chamber of commerce approached MCI Long Distance, hoping one of their managers could train chamber members in telemarketing. Understandably, MCI, following typical corporate logic of that era, declined to allocate a manager's time for this endeavor, as they had their own employees to train. Instead, they recommended that the chamber reach out to me, as I was in the process of starting my own business. Did I have the time? Not really. Did I need the exposure? Absolutely.

The chamber of commerce contacted me and requested my assistance in conducting training sessions. I agreed, but there was one caveat.

"I'd be happy to help," I told the chamber representative over the phone, "but there's one condition."

"What's that?" she asked.

"I need to become a chamber member to do this."

"Of course! We can set that up right away."

"Well"—I paused—"the membership dues don't exactly fit my budget right now. What if we did a trade instead? I'll provide the training in exchange for a membership."

There was silence on the other end, then, "Let me call you back."

Two hours later, my phone rang.

"Sharon? We've never done this before, but the board approved it. You've got yourself a deal."

I became the one and only trade at the Austin Chamber of Commerce, an incredible break for The Upstairs Maid. This opportunity allowed me to stand before forty to fifty diverse individuals every week for three months, teaching them the art of phone sales, excuse me, the art of telemarketing. Considering that this topic isn't the most exciting, akin to discussing Robert's Rules of Order (which I happen to have three credits in), I was pleasantly surprised by the high attendance. I meticulously prepared each presentation, and I must say, I excelled. After all, I majored in speech with a focus on rhetoric and public address. This stint was my coming-out party as Sharon Butza, the face behind The Upstairs Maid.

I genuinely believe that community involvement is the cornerstone of small service businesses. It offers free advertising, establishes immediate identity and credibility, and provides various forms of support. Engaging with your community, especially as a small business with limited capital, is an excellent way to foster growth. Through such involvement, you encounter attorneys, doctors, chiropractors, community leaders, and potential investors.

You become well-informed about local developments and gain an edge when investing in real estate. This independence from real-estate agents, who can sometimes prioritize their interests over yours, is a valuable long-term benefit. Immediate rewards include gaining easy access to answers and experiencing business growth. It's important to remember that attending a chamber luncheon won't immediately lead to a flurry of phone calls, but it does yield long-term advantages. You reap what you sow.

After my summer of telemarketing training concluded, so did my free advertising through the chamber. Many homeowners in Austin had now heard of The Upstairs Maid, but I knew my free ride had ended. Despite this, I continued my chamber involvement and explored other cost-effective ways to promote my business.

My continued participation involved volunteering for an unpopular task: membership outreach. This task was quite similar to telemarketing. We would call chamber members to gauge their satisfaction, a task few relished because many members felt they weren't getting enough value from their membership. It was tempting to remind them that they received what they invested, but I wisely refrained from such commentary to maintain The Upstairs Maid's image. Instead, I listened to their grievances and thanked them for their input. Volunteering may not have directly earned money for my business, but it was a remarkable way to brand our company name without spending money.

I always began these calls the same way: "Hello, I am Sharon Butza, and today I am calling on behalf of the chamber of commerce. In my other life, I own The Upstairs Maid."

This opened the door for both conversations. While I never actively promoted The Upstairs Maid during these calls, I did provide my number and explained that calls would be answered as The Upstairs Maid because I was volunteering. Although I didn't make any sales for The Upstairs Maid during these calls, I did receive inquiries and eventually converted them into sales.

I meticulously logged every phone call and documented the feedback. Although I didn't discuss these calls during committee meetings, I submitted written reports. My performance exceeded the chamber's goals for committee members in terms of monthly contacts, and I never missed a meeting. In some months, I was the only committee member who made any calls, let alone surpassing our target by 50 percent. The following year, I became the chair of that committee, and within two years, I was appointed to the Northwest Chamber Board. Two more years passed, and I became chair of the Northwest Chamber, leading every monthly luncheon.

That role changed something important. When meetings were small, everyone could stand up and introduce themselves. People heard your name once, maybe twice. But as attendance grew, from 30 people to 150, and eventually even larger, there wasn't time for everyone to speak. Introductions became limited. That's when I experienced the real power of being introduced by someone else instead of introducing myself. A board member would introduce me as the chamber president before each luncheon; and throughout the meeting, my company name, The Upstairs Maid, came up again and again as I facilitated, made announcements, and guided the room.

It was the same principle I had used in sales: Repetition builds familiarity, and familiarity builds trust. In the early days, no one knew who I was, so I made repeated calls for the chamber ambassador committee. I showed up repeatedly. I had repeated conversations, repeated lunches, repeated meetings. Over time, the group grew, my visibility grew with it, and so did the recognition of my company's name. By the end of my term as president, thousands of people had heard my name, seen my face, or shaken my hand, often multiple times. When they later needed their homes cleaned, The Upstairs Maid wasn't a stranger. We were a familiar name. Networking wasn't about showing up once; it was about showing up repeatedly, in a way that made your name and your business feel known long before someone needed your service.

That idea of repeated exposure didn't just apply to people, it applied to events as well. Around that time, progressive dinners were becoming popular, where guests moved from home to home for different courses. Watching how that format kept people engaged and connected gave me an idea for how we could make chamber luncheons more dynamic and draw larger crowds.

In the nineties, progressive dinners gained popularity. These dinners entailed having appetizers at one friend's home, moving to another home for salads, and so on, much like a culinary adventure. Back then, DWIs were seldom issued, which contributed to their success. I would recommend modernizing this concept by ordering an SUV Lyft to shuttle between homes, as DWI regulations are much stricter today, but progressive dinners are too much fun to give up.

I applied the concept of progressive dinners to our chamber luncheons. Attendees had their salad with one table, their entrée with another table, and dessert with the final table. Instead of mingling with just eight people at a luncheon, attendees could now interact with twenty-four. It was an ingenious modification that worked splendidly for our members, and we even had to turn people away due to sold-out events. While it was fun, it required extensive planning before each luncheon. I assigned numbers to tables for attendees to start at and switch to, ensuring a smooth transition. As I mentioned earlier, we consistently sold out our luncheons.

As chair of the Northwest Chamber, I also had a seat on the Greater Austin Chamber Board. During the early 1990s, The Upstairs Maid was the most prominent cleaning service known in the chamber. A couple of other cleaning services held memberships but remained largely inactive. In those days, you could find around eighty cleaning services listed in the Yellow Pages, and websites were just beginning to emerge in the last quarter of my twenty years, with worldwide searches not exceeding one billion until 2005. My chamber position provided a cost-effective and highly effective means of branding our company.

The chamber isn't the sole means of promoting your business. Any form of community service volunteering is an excellent way to enhance your company's visibility. Advertising can be extraordinarily expensive and not always effective. Some individuals spend substantial sums on advertising merely to satisfy their egos by seeing their name in print. Personally, I place significant trust in numbers. I advocate tracking everything without hesitation and making decisions based upon those tracking, although there may be instances when your intuition tells you otherwise. It's crucial to start with accurate data before considering gut feelings. Allow me to illustrate this point.

When I initially assumed control of The Upstairs Maid, income statements and budgets were foreign to me. I had earned well in the corporate world, providing me with the means to buy whatever I desired. I had never prepared a personal budget, so business finances were uncharted territory. I had previously worked as a sales manager, and like most in that position, I continued to expand my knowledge in that area. My former VP of sales at MCI Long Distance once distributed a small paperback book on business finances, urging us to comprehend our department's income statements. Unfortunately, none of us ever bothered to read that book. Now, in retrospect, I wish I had, as I often had to refer to it during those early startup days. Managing finances in my own business left me with far less time than I enjoyed during my corporate career.

Initially, I tracked very little because I didn't know what to monitor. There were no industry organizations, no Google, and no advice to rely on. I frequently told Keri, my office manager, that we were "making things up as we go," and indeed, that's precisely what we did. Consequently, we made our fair share of mistakes. One such oversight was failing to ask prospects how they heard about us when they called for a quote. At the time, I had minimal advertising running, and I assumed I knew how people were finding us since I was the only one answering the phones for the first two years. Unfortunately, asking this critical question never became a habit for me. I started doing so only after I began investing what I considered substantial sums of money in advertising, which was roughly three years into the business.

When we finally started tracking the source of our calls, we were in for a significant revelation. At one point, I decided to invest $1,000 in a single advertisement, taking pride in securing a full back-page placement in a magazine. I eagerly ran the ad in mid-August and anxiously waited for the phones to ring off the hook. To my surprise, they did. But more of a surprise was the statistical fact that when August ended, there was not a single sale attributed to that magazine ad. I reasoned that perhaps September would fare better, but once again, it yielded only one isolated sale. It became evident that our corner of the home-service businesses, residential cleaning services, would naturally grow during August, September, and October, regardless of advertising efforts. This was the period each year when I would typically expand the number of teams. Don't get me wrong, advertising in August is essential, and it can undoubtedly boost sales. My point is that, you will not know if a particular advertisement produces results if you do not ask and track, and it's best to abandon it immediately if it is not producing results. We continued tracking the source of every single call for the next seventeen years, allowing us to determine what worked and when to run specific ads.

What continues to surprise me is how few service business owners, even today, consistently ask new clients how they heard about them. It's such a simple question, and yet it's often overlooked. On the rare occasion someone has asked me that as a customer, I've been impressed. My immediate thought was, they must run a tight operation if they're paying attention to where their business is coming from. It's also a natural icebreaker. There's nothing awkward about asking, "Do you mind if I ask how you heard about us?" If they say, "A friend referred me," that opens the door to say, "That's wonderful, would you mind telling me who? I'd love to send them a thank-you." And then you send one. That's how relationships grow. That's how referrals become repeatable.

Some owners tell me, "People don't remember anyway." Sometimes that's true. But sometimes it isn't, and you'll never know unless you ask. Even imperfect data is better than no data.

For years, whenever I held events where people registered for free cleanings, I included questions like, "Have you heard of us before?" and "If yes, how?" I even listed things like billboards just to see what people would say. I've never done a billboard in my life, yet every now and then someone would check that box. It made me laugh, but statistically, it was insignificant, maybe two out of a hundred. It didn't distort the bigger picture at all. What it did was remind me that tracking doesn't have to be perfect to be useful.

Where and how you spend your money matters too much to leave to guesswork. Advertising, networking, referrals—none of it should be based on hope alone. If you don't know what's working, you can't repeat it. And if you can't repeat it, you can't build predictable growth.

Building relationships with day-care centers and schools at all levels is an excellent way to gain favorable exposure for your company. Any support you offer to parents and children will yield returns many times over. Programs like Partners in Education, if available in your school district, provide an avenue for involvement. These programs connect businesses with public schools, offering support in various forms. In return, businesses receive coverage in school publications or exposure at school events, effectively placing their names in front of hundreds of busy parents. Most Partners in Education programs are facilitated by local chambers of commerce, so it's a good idea to start by contacting your chamber. They match businesses with schools and oversee the year-long partnerships. I was on the founding board for a school district that adopted this program, an excellent exposure opportunity for The Upstairs Maid. During my involvement, I collaborated with high-level business executives who, incidentally, did not clean their own homes. Meeting me led them to enlist my services, often times replacing a nondependable solo cleaner they heard about through a friend. I never explicitly mentioned my profession but was often asked what I did for a living and my answer often resulted in a request that I contact their wives directly. At this level, I would personally reach out to the wives before passing them on to Keri or Nancy.

Partners in Education typically asked businesses to provide mentors for at-risk students, a rewarding experience indeed. I became a mentor for a child, and our school weekly visits relationship lasted for three years. Eventually, it blossomed into a lifelong connection. Beth, my mentee, has grown into a kind, intelligent, generous, and successful woman. The experience was rewarding for both of us, and it resulted in repeat clients who had met me through the program and trusted my company. Participants in Partners in Education programs are typically vetted for working with children, ensuring the safety of the students involved. If you're running a small company with limited time and resources, offering free cleanings to exceptional teachers or mentors of at-risk students might be the ideal form of involvement. Many schoolteachers, like radio announcers, are often underpaid and underappreciated in many school districts. I vividly recall listening to a news report during a city council meeting in St. Louis in 2023 where the topic of raising teachers' salaries from $36,000 to $38,000 per year was being debated. It was a shockingly low figure. Conversely, I had just left the office of a cleaning service where the cleaners were earning an average of $1,000 per week. I'll refrain from delving into this issue here, but it highlights the importance of valuing and supporting our nation's educators. Despite receiving minimal compensation, teachers are highly regarded. In fact, one year, I provided biweekly services for an entire year to the Teacher of the Year. Previously, they had received nothing more than a bouquet of roses as an acknowledgment. At the annual awards dinner, where I presented the gift, I received a standing ovation from the attendees. Another client in Kennesaw, Georgia, had a similar experience when they honored their Teacher of the Year with free repeat cleanings. We both gained repeat clients from that single donation. If you're seeking ways to support your local schools, I suggest reaching out to them directly and inquiring about how you can assist. Private schools are a great place to start, and the parents most likely do not clean their own homes.

What these experiences taught me, whether through chambers, schools, or community programs, was that visibility alone isn't enough. Being present opens doors, but relationships are what keep them open. Over time, I began to understand that growth didn't come from showing up everywhere; it came from showing up well. Trust, credibility, and connection didn't happen by accident. They required intention, consistency, and a willingness to step beyond comfort. That realization marked a shift for me, from simply participating in organizations to deliberately building relationships within them.

CHAPTER 4

BUILDING BRIDGES AND RELATIONSHIPS

Networking, the art of forging connections and cultivating relationships, can often feel like a second job. It's a commitment that may not always be the most enticing prospect, especially for those new to the experience. Some days, scrubbing a toilet seems more appealing than attending another networking event. The challenge is amplified when you venture solo into an event for the first time, where you know no one. Over the years, I've encountered numerous such situations, but I've developed techniques that have made networking more manageable and allowed me to break through the "inner circle glass ceiling."

The linchpin of successful networking lies in the profound understanding that "first impressions are lasting impressions." Dressing appropriately is pivotal. Successful business owners don attire that befits their status, setting them apart from employees. While a polo shirt with your company name may gain you quick recognition, it may inadvertently convey that you are still entrenched in day-to-day operations. Clients want a partner who will remain a fixture for the long haul, someone they can trust with access to their homes. They've witnessed countless startups come and go. Statistics show that four out of five startups close within the first five years. Clients also prefer a service provider who appears prosperous enough to cover any potential damages or losses. Present yourself as a successful individual, akin to a banker, albeit without the same mindset.

Carry business cards, but don't treat them like confetti. The goal isn't to hand out the most cards in the room; it's to hand one to someone who remembers who you are when they look at it later and choose to keep it. That part is up to you. A business card only works if it represents a real interaction, not a rushed exchange.

Sharing contact information by text can be helpful, but it doesn't replace connection. For a first networking event, my approach is simple: Find one person you can comfortably spend forty-five minutes talking with, someone you genuinely like or wouldn't mind getting to know. Finding that person early takes the pressure off and turns networking into a conversation instead of a performance.

How do you identify someone open to conversing and forming a connection? Look for individuals who intermittently engage in conversations but also spend time alone during the event. When approached, they greet others warmly, chat briefly, and then gracefully move on. Try to befriend such individuals. Introduce yourself and remember the 5Ws that form the foundation of successful networking:

Who: Gather the courage to introduce yourself and offer a handshake.

What: Ask about their profession or what brought them to the event.

How: Inquire about their professional journey.

Where: Ask about their place of origin or whether they have always lived in your city.

When: If the event involves seating, use this as an opportunity to ask about the ideal time for selecting seats.

At this juncture, you've shared little about yourself unless they express interest. Remember, people tend to linger when they feel heard. Utilize your two ears and one mouth wisely. Demonstrating genuine interest in others is a surefire way to win their favor. If executed adeptly, you might just find a networking companion for the next event or, at the very least, a dinner companion for this event. Goal achieved. Keep an eye on the seating arrangements. If seats start to fill up, inquire about dinner promptly to reserve two adjacent spots. After the event, plan to meet for lunch or cocktails to further solidify your connection before the next networking event.

Within a year, you should be able to ascertain whether the organization is a worthwhile investment of your time and resources, offering the potential for acquiring repeat clients and a range of supplementary benefits. If it doesn't yield mutual benefits, you cannot justify continued involvement. Although philanthropy is commendable, practical decisions should be based on the fundamental principle: "If it doesn't make money, it doesn't make sense." Networking must yield repeat clients to replace advertising costs, especially if you're just starting out.

After twelve years of networking with the chamber, I must admit I got tired of it. I occasionally attended events, but I'd been on every committee I wanted to serve, president of one of the five chambers, and sat on the downtown board. I felt I had very little enthusiasm to give the chamber anymore and very little for me to gain. A friend and my insurance agent suggested I try the organization that owned the Caswell House. The house was named after the family that built it in 1900. It was one of the cleaning jobs we received from our purchase of The Upstairs Maid for $30,000 ten years earlier. Over those ten years, the Caswell House paid us back for the $30K we paid for our entire business.

In 1996, the Austin Junior Forum (AJF) had about sixty members, all females, who were quite powerful women in the city of Austin. Every now and then they would get on a roll and complain about the quality of our cleanings, and I would have to go to the house and listen to some rude woman tell me what we had done wrong when cleaning the home. At this time, I was very active in the Austin Chamber and the Women's Chamber Board, so I wasn't really intimidated by these people, but they certainly treated me like I was. My parents paid for my entire college education, so joining a sorority was not an option for me, and they were an adult sorority, in my opinion.

I was on the Women's Chamber Board with a young woman who was also very active in AJF. I asked her to lunch one day and, toward the end of lunch, asked her if there was a reason why she never asked me to join AJF.

"Oh my gosh," she said, setting down her fork. "I thought you were far too busy to do that. I would love to sponsor you."

And that was the start of a decade of personal growth for me and financial growth for The Upstairs Maid.

I was shocked by the fact that AJF was always looking for members, but I was still very excited about going to my first meeting. I was nine plus years into our business, so we had close to $1 million gross income. Comfortable, but not as rich as most of the women I was about to network with. I had my hair styled and took a lot of time choosing my outfit for my first AJF event. I had some experience with some of the sustaining members who complained about our cleanings, and that led to my profiling the type of woman I expected to meet that night. All of this was very new to me, but they operated like I would suspect a sorority would operate. I was to be a prospective member for the first year, and then there was an inauguration meeting where I would become a regular member. I learned very quickly that these women had very cliquey little groups, which brought my thoughts back to some of my not-so-good memories of high school. I was a farmer's daughter. I was country when country wasn't cool. Now I was joining an organization full of previous sorority members who are now CEO, banker, director, and VP's wives. I own a home-service business and am still actively working on it. What was I thinking?

The first meeting was difficult. I found one person I could talk to who looked as lost as I felt. This young lady had just married into a very well-known and wealthy car dealership family in Austin. Because of my chamber background, I was able to chat with her about the community. She and I were tolerating this event for the same reason: to meet people who might buy a car or have their home cleaned by one of our companies. I didn't bond with anyone other than her, but that was okay because she was also a prospective, and I now knew someone I could sit with at the next event. Goal attained.

In November, we had what was called Christmas at Caswell, a ten-day event that generated a lot of net income for our organization to give to women and children in need. AJF was a very upscale organization compared to any other organization I had belonged to thus far. Many of the members were college graduates who could take as much time as they wanted on any project they took on. They did not work. They had individual cleaners for their homes, and some had cooks. They were extremely blessed women who felt an obligation to give back to the community. Women and children tug at any woman's heart, especially those who have never struggled. Several of the younger members were daughters of what they called sustainers, women who used to belong to the organization but are now in their senior years and have outgrown the desire to volunteer in an organized fashion. It was truly time for a younger crowd to take over if we were going to continue to be a voice in the community. I was forty-eight when I joined, and change was clearly overdue.

The enchanting "Christmas at Caswell" event unfolded within the historic walls of the Caswell House, a property owned and utilized by AJF for fundraising and committee meetings. This captivating tale finds its roots in 1972 when the city, having deemed the house unfit, decided to put it up for sale due to its occupation by drug addicts and the ensuing safety hazards posed to the affluent families residing nearby.

Five remarkable women, driven by a passion to assist women and children in need, had already established AJF and were witnessing its rapid growth. Recognizing the need for a dedicated meeting place and sufficient funds to truly impact the lives of those in need, they turned their eyes toward the Caswell House. This splendid abode not only met their requirements but also offered the opportunity to preserve its architectural grandeur through renovations.

With a meticulously prepared business plan, the five visionary women embarked on a mission to secure a loan. It was 1972, and they were five women, so after initial rejections, they enlisted the support of their husbands, who agreed to cosign for the loan. Suddenly, the very first bank they had approached saw the potential in their idea. These five pioneering women acquired the Caswell House for $90,000 and embarked on its restoration. They authored a cookbook, followed by a second edition, with every penny generated being channeled back into the restoration effort. Remarkably, they managed to pay off the house in just five years.

"Christmas at Caswell" was conceived as a means to generate funds for aiding women and children in need, the very essence for which AJF was established. Their foresight proved to be astute, as the Caswell House now serves as the venue for all AJF meetings and is even rented out for weddings and other events, continuing to give back to the community.

While these five women may have ascended to heaven, their indomitable spirits left an indelible mark on countless lives. It was an honor to have known, worked alongside, and, on occasion, been reprimanded by these remarkable women. Their influence on my life, particularly in reshaping my perceptions of individuals with wealth, endures forever. Wealthy individuals, like all others, deserve to be judged as individuals, not merely based on their financial status.

As prospective members, we were required to volunteer for twenty hours during the "Christmas at Caswell" event, our largest fundraiser of the year. Preparations for this extravaganza spanned an entire year, culminating in a spectacular ten-day celebration. With approximately twenty events to choose from for our volunteer hours, I was both surprised and delighted to discover numerous opportunities to serve as a luncheon hostess, all of which were available. This role allowed me to don my finest attire and seat guests, sparing me from dishwashing or food-plating duties, which carried the risk of spilling something on a client during meal service.

The week preceding "Christmas at Caswell" involved the collective effort of the entire organization to prepare the house for the forthcoming ten-day extravaganza. We transformed this majestic old mansion into a winter wonderland, a formidable task considering the sunshine and mideighties temperatures outside. During that week, all prospective were mandated to contribute eight hours of their time. Themes were chosen, and each decorator would design one room on the first floor in alignment with the chosen theme. The second floor housed a ballroom and a small galley kitchen, where we would plate lunches and serve the public. Meanwhile, the basement was transformed into a bustling gift shop.

For my eight-hour commitment in the week leading up to "Christmas at Caswell," I opted to assist in the basement's gift shop. Upon entering the room, I noticed that my presence hardly registered amidst the hustle and bustle of the women laboring tirelessly to transform the basement into a winter wonderland. Eventually, one of the sustaining members handed me a collection of Christmas items and instructed me to decorate a wall, the very first wall a visitor would encounter upon descending the basement steps.

"Just arrange these on the wall in a way that makes people want to buy them," she said, gesturing vaguely.

My mission was to arrange these items on the wall in a manner that would beckon anyone to purchase them. Despite my doubts, I devoted eight hours to this task, completing my full shift. I left the room that day feeling a sense of pride in the wall I had fashioned.

In my earnest desire to make a favorable impression, I returned to the gift shop the following day to offer further assistance. As I descended those very steps, my eyes beheld a wall that was entirely unrecognizable. It had undergone a complete transformation. The woman who had assigned me the task approached me, her eyes undoubtedly catching the emotional turmoil evident on my face.

"Sharon, I'm so sorry about the changes," she said softly.

I forced a smile. "No, I completely understand. If I possessed the decorating talent, I would have made the same choice."

I lent a hand in unpacking additional Christmas items for sale before excusing myself.

"I need to get back to the office," I said and left.

I would love to say this part of the journey felt inspiring, but it didn't. It was exhausting. Emotionally draining. There were days I would have rather scrubbed nineteen toilets than walk into another event with the Austin Junior Forum and feel invisible all over again. I knew this group mattered. I knew it was key to building the kind of repeat, high-trust relationships our business needed. But simply being present wasn't enough. Showing up without a clear purpose just made me tired, not effective.

What I began to understand was that growth in these rooms, just like in business, had to be intentional and repeatable. It wasn't about attending once or twice and hoping something would click. It was about finding a role, a contribution, and a way to be seen and remembered, then doing that consistently over time. Relationships didn't grow from effort alone; they grew from repeated, meaningful engagement. If I was going to stay in that world, I had to change how I showed up, not just be there but become someone the group could rely on and recognize.

That decision didn't take long to test. The day I had eagerly anticipated had arrived. "Christmas at Caswell" was not just a fundraiser in name; it was a remarkably well-orchestrated operation. The luncheon, which drew hundreds of women each day, was made possible because caterers donated the food, one complete luncheon per day, delivered on trays directly to the kitchen. Because there was no food cost, every ticket sold translated almost entirely into fundraising revenue. Women from the Caswell House and Austin Junior Forum worked in the kitchen, carefully plating each dish and making it look beautiful, while members served the meals to guests. After a less-than-welcoming experience at the spring welcome event and the gift-shop debacle, I was finally ready to put on my red power suit and step into the role of the "hostess with the mostest" at "Christmas at Caswell."

The Caswell House opened its doors at 10:00 a.m. for visitors to shop, and the dining room commenced by serving lunch at 11:15 a.m. On the day of my shift, I arrived in the basement to sign in promptly at 10:30 a.m., then proceeded upstairs to the dining room. To my surprise, there was already a line of ladies waiting on the stairs to be seated. By the time the tables were set and the food was ready to be plated in the kitchen, a long line of ladies extended out the front door, onto the front porch, down the steps, and onto the sidewalk. I quickly learned that when women came to the Caswell House for lunch, they made a beeline for the top of the stairs. By 11:15 a.m., we had arranged the place settings and glasses on the tables, and I was finally able to start seating the first group of ninety women. It was incredibly enjoyable. The women were brimming with excitement, and it was evident that they adored this event. Some of them even expressed their gratitude for my volunteer efforts and complimented my power suit. For about twenty minutes, I felt like I was in heaven on earth. However, when I returned to my lectern at the top of the stairs, I gazed upon a seemingly endless line of ladies still waiting to be seated. Some had been standing in line for forty to fifty minutes and hadn't made it to the first seating. Their mood took a downturn when they realized they had another hour to wait before the current seating finished, the tables were turned, and they could finally be seated.

It quickly turned into a nightmare. I stood at the top of the stairs listening to irritated individuals berating the system, deeming it inefficient and ignorant. Some even declared that they would never return. I can remember thinking that they were ruder than some of my clients back at the office, and I was volunteering. At least, I got paid there. I needed a solution that would not only pacify the waiting guests but also provide relief for myself. As soon as a table became available, I took it upon myself to reset it and seat the next group in line. This deviated from the established policy, but I decided to adhere to one of my favorite principles that "It is easier to ask for forgiveness than permission." I continued turning tables. By 2:15 p.m., we had to close, leaving some of the guests in line without lunch. Another unfortunate outcome was that none of them spent money in the gift shop since they had dedicated all their time to standing in line. Exhausted and overwhelmed, I returned to my office, wondering how I would endure four more days of this. It became apparent why I was the sole person who had volunteered to be a hostess.

That night, I slept very little, not because I was nervous about speaking up but because I kept replaying the chaos in my head and thinking through how it could be fixed. By morning, I knew exactly what needed to change. What I didn't fully understand yet was how much leverage I had. The job I was doing was miserable, thankless, and no one else wanted it. If I walked away, they would be stuck figuring it out themselves, and they knew it.

The next day, I approached the registration desk and spoke plainly. I made sure they understood that the problem wasn't personal.

"Yesterday was a disaster," I said. "Not because of you, but because the system doesn't work. I think I can fix it."

They listened more carefully than I expected. Looking back, I don't think it was because they were impressed by me. I think it was because they were relieved someone was willing to take ownership of a job no one else wanted.

"I'll seat the first ninety people in line the way it's always been done," I explained. "But after that, I want to give everyone numbers. That way they can walk through the house or shop instead of standing in line. I'll clear tables as they open, walk the rooms, and find the next numbers."

There was hesitation. One woman crossed her arms. "We've never done it that way."

"I know," I said. "But we can't have people standing in line for an hour and then leaving without spending money. That hurts everyone."

They exchanged glances. Finally, one of them nodded. "All right," she said. "Try it."

At the time, I thought they were doing me a favor. Later, I realized something far more important: When you're willing to do the hard, unpopular work, and do it well, people are far more flexible than they let on.

The new system worked wonderfully. The guests were thrilled when I approached them with their numbers, ready to seat them. The positive feedback I received contrasted starkly with the previous day's nightmare. On the fourth day, they asked me to hostess for the full ten days, and surprisingly, I had a great time doing it. I had become an indispensable part of AJF, particularly "Christmas at Caswell," and I was treated accordingly. I also managed to shed twelve pounds over those ten days due to the constant running up and down the stairs. This event marked the beginning of my daily exercise routine, which I continue to this day. Thanks to my idea of seating guests more efficiently, "Christmas at Caswell's" gift shop raked in an additional $15,000 in net sales. The week turned out to be enjoyable and successful, but the most rewarding aspect was that this event had a tremendous impact on branding The Upstairs Maid. The name became well-known among the affluent women of Austin, even though I only mentioned it when asked.

The following year, I was automatically selected to be the hostess. My name was written in for the position even before the schedule was distributed among active members. Motorola generously donated eight walkie-talkies for our use during the event, enabling me to simply announce the numbers while the floor managers relayed them to the diners. This innovative change greatly enhanced our efficiency. I can't help but chuckle when I write about walkie-talkies. Do they even still make them?

I had also pushed for phone reservations at the "Christmas at Caswell" wrap-up meeting, as Internet reservations were not yet an option. Securing the walkie-talkies had been seen as a significant achievement, and my idea was not accepted. I took it upon myself to inform everyone I seated that year we would be taking reservations the following year. Back to my usual MO: "It's easier to ask for forgiveness than permission." The following year we were allowed to take reservations. I volunteered to manage the reservations, knowing it would significantly simplify the process and provide me with an opportunity to engage with those making reservations. Managing 270 people per day, many of whom reserved spots in groups of 4 to 8, seemed like a breeze considering the fact we were booking 50 to 55 jobs per day at The Upstairs Maid at this time.

To my surprise, I was also appointed as the chairperson of the catering committee. It was highly unusual for such a key position to be given to a prospective member. "Christmas at Caswell" was gaining even more popularity, especially among the business crowd, thanks to the reservation system. Securing the caterers turned out to be surprisingly easy, whereas managing reservations was quite overwhelming due to the constant influx. Incredibly, I managed to book most of the lunches before opening day. We shifted to numbering tables and seating guests according to the seating chart. It worked beautifully. I made only one scheduling error, arranging for 3,300 people to be seated. That year, "Christmas at Caswell" raised an impressive $85,000 net, and I received a fair share of commendations.

The subsequent year, I was asked to take on the role of "Christmas at Caswell" chair, coinciding with the one hundredth-year anniversary of the Caswell House in 2000. The prospect of leading this milestone event filled me with immense excitement. During that year, I managed reservations and sold every seat before opening day, started Spanish classes at Austin Community College, the business hit $1.2M; and we embarked on the construction of our new house. It was undoubtedly one of the best years of my life. "Christmas at Caswell" managed to raise an astonishing $110,000 net, setting a new benchmark.

AJF had become my life, shaping my friendships and contributing to my income. We were cleaning nearly half of the members' homes. Another 25 percent of our repeat sales came from exposure within AJF. I made appearances on television multiple times, was referred by members to their friends, and within five years, we were able to stop accepting one-time cleaning requests. AJF had played a pivotal role in the growth of our company, focusing on repeat cleaning services.

Because of my intense involvement in AJF, I was quite well-known and found myself consistently appointed to the nominating committee each year. While serving on the nominating committee, I gained insights into discussions about potential future presidents. Regrettably, it became evident that my name was never put forward as a contender for the presidential position, leaving me somewhat perplexed as to the reasons behind this omission. Consequently, following my tenure as the "Christmas at Caswell" chair, like the chamber, I perceived that I had fully explored my potential within the organization. I began to adopt a more reserved approach, restricting my engagement to the minimal requirements for maintaining my active status and decided to assume the role of sustainer, with its prerequisite of twenty hours of annual volunteer work. I volunteered 1,400 hours per year to AJF. It was a welcome respite to finally have some time to myself, albeit a brief time.

Shockingly, one evening, I answered the phone to hear, "Are you sitting down?" Shelli Hill was on the line and humorously said, "I get to call you because you once called me, if you recall, and talked me into being AJF president. Now it's my turn. We want you to be president."

I was taken aback by the offer. The only explanation I could fathom was perhaps my absence from active participation had kept me out of any recent disagreements or differences of opinion among the members. Ultimately, I chose to accept the position. With the amazing support of my membership chair, Demetra, our membership grew from 60 members to 160. Each gathering at the Caswell House was a memorable affair, thanks to Demetra's premeeting cocktail and appetizer social hours that kept members returning. Demetra and I had an exceptional year. We could always rely on each other to fulfill every commitment we made. Another confirmation of the necessity and value of a strong leadership team.

My position as president of AJF brought me numerous more appearances on television, a welcome development. I had lost my radio advocate who started her own business. So my own personal appearance on TV at the right times was crucial. AJF had indeed become my primary source of branding and, subsequently, income.

CHAPTER 5

LEVERAGING FREE TELEVISION ADVERTISING

Television advertising, a venture many companies explore, is not a path I found particularly lucrative, as it entails exorbitant costs, especially if you aim to make it your primary branding strategy. One of the main drawbacks is that more often than not your expensive commercial airs when viewers typically step away to grab a snack from the refrigerator, rendering your investment less effective. However, I discovered a novel approach to secure valuable airtime on television without shelling out a dime, a method that allowed me to reach an engaged audience during peak viewing hours.

Throughout the twenty years our company existed, I had the privilege of appearing on television a remarkable nineteen times. More remarkably, my inaugural television appearance had nothing to do with my business or my involvement in the community. It all began during the lead-up to my first wedding when I encountered an unexpected setback.

As our wedding day drew near, I was seated in my office when our five part-time cleaning employees rushed in, their excitement palpable.

"Sharon! Sharon!" they called out breathlessly. "The shop where you bought your wedding dress—it's closed!"

I looked up from my paperwork. "What do you mean closed?"

"We drove by there today. The doors are locked, and there's a sign on the window."

I felt my stomach drop. "But my dress is there. It's being altered."

"We know," one of them said sympathetically.

I was incredulous. My wedding dress was currently at the shop for alterations, along with the fabric for the bridesmaids' dresses. Attempting to contact the shop proved futile: Their phone line was temporarily disconnected. With my mother visiting from Wisconsin, we decided to take matters into our own hands. Upon arriving at the wedding boutique, we were met with a scene of disgruntled brides, all demanding access to their dresses. The shop remained locked, its curtains drawn. I joined the protest, driven by my upbringing, which instilled a strong sense of standing up for my rights. It wasn't long before TV cameras arrived; and I, evidently captivating TV fodder, was interviewed. This incident marked my first television appearance.

Meanwhile, I had no wedding dress. My seamstress called me and informed me she managed to retrieve my fabric and informed me that the boutique's owner still operated a shop in San Antonio, despite filing for chapter 13 bankruptcy. To ensure the legality of my plan, I consulted an attorney I had met at a networking event. Armed with my canceled check as evidence, I hatched a plan to secure a replacement dress. It was a time when the Internet was not yet ubiquitous. Canceled checks were still physically mailed by the USPS. The check had already been cashed and returned to me, as expected. My plan was straightforward: I would enter the San Antonio store, select a dress similar to the one I had purchased, and walk out with it.

The seamstress had mentioned that the San Antonio store had limited opening hours, which was another challenge because San Antonio is an hour- and-a-half-hour drive on a good traffic day, one way. Managing a start-up company and planning a wedding little time left for wasted trips to a closed shop. I consulted a Crisscross Directory for San Antonio and found a phone number for a home right next to the address of the wedding store. Unlike today, where phone calls frequently go unanswered, my call was promptly picked up. A kind, elderly voice answered, "Hello."

I explained my wedding dress predicament, concluding by mentioning that the seamstress had informed me that the store operated on limited hours. In an act of great kindness, this gracious lady walked across the street, jotted down the store's hours of operation, and called me back with the information.

On the next available day, we promptly arrived in front of the San Antonio establishment, clutching my wedding dress receipt. Inside, I located a suitable dress.

I was unsurprisingly halted by a vigilant clerk who questioned my actions.

"Excuse me, what are you doing?" she demanded.

I calmly displayed my canceled check. "I already paid for a dress at your Austin location. This is proof. I'm taking this dress."

The clerk's face turned red. "You can't just take that! I'm calling the police!"

I shrugged. "Go ahead. I'll wait right here."

Unperturbed, I welcomed their arrival, but the clerk decided to call the owner first. The owner called their attorney, and about thirty minutes later, I was able to leave with the wedding dress. I must confess, I couldn't help but constantly glance at the back seat to admire the dress all the way home. I had pulled off quite the feat. Looking back, I might have missed an opportunity for further television exposure by not following up and sharing the remainder of the story with the press.

Yet my efforts to secure free advertising didn't stop there. I engineered my next appearance without any networking connections or outside help, relying entirely on my own initiative, except for securing a location for the shoot. At the time, Bill Clinton was attempting to gain Senate approval for his nominee for attorney general, Zoë Baird. Her nomination was historic: Female candidates for such high-level government roles were still rare. The nomination unraveled, however, when it was revealed that she had employed an undocumented worker as her personal cleaner, an issue that quickly became national news.

At that point in history, the conversation around undocumented workers was still in its infancy, especially when it came to private homes. Many Americans, myself included, were only beginning to understand that undocumented labor even existed outside of agriculture. In Texas, undocumented workers were more commonly associated with seasonal farm labor, sometimes arriving legally during harvest periods. But employing undocumented workers inside private residences was different. It raised questions about legality, accountability, communication, and safety. I had made a deliberate decision to hire only documented workers who could communicate in English, and at the time, I was among the last cleaning companies in Austin to do so. That decision set us apart. My concern wasn't political; it was practical. If the attorney general of the United States could be approved after employing undocumented household help, it risked sending a message that this practice was acceptable everywhere. For a business like mine, built on trust inside people's homes, that precedent mattered.

Before email, before social media, I sat down at my electric typewriter and wrote a letter explaining exactly that. I outlined why approving an attorney general who had employed undocumented household workers could unintentionally encourage similar behavior nationwide. I faxed the letter to every local television station using the fax machine we kept in the office closet, then waited.

Within four hours of transmitting my message, a television station contacted me, eager to interview me on this hot topic.

"Ms. Butza, this is Jennifer from Channel 7 News. We received your fax about the Zoë Baird situation."

My heart raced. "Yes?"

"We'd like to interview you for our evening broadcast. Would you be available this afternoon?"

"Absolutely," I said, trying to keep my voice steady.

"Great. Do you have a location where we could film? Ideally somewhere that shows your business in action?"

My excitement knew no bounds: This marked my first official appearance on TV promoting The Upstairs Maid. To facilitate the interview, I reached out to one of my less-favored clients, as I needed a suitable location. The TV station preferred to conduct interviews in a client's home, as it allowed them to showcase cleaning activities in the background. While my home was adequate, it hardly showcased the grandeur I wished to convey to the community about our cleaning services. However, Heather Watson, the founder of the Women's Chamber of Commerce in Austin, had been a client of mine for some time. I had also been servicing her home weekly.

"Rose, I have an unusual request," I said when I called her.

"What is it, Sharon?"

"Channel 7 wants to interview me about the Zoë Baird situation, and they want to film at a client's home with my team cleaning in the background. Would you be willing to host?"

"Are you kidding?" Heather laughed. "This is perfect! I can promote the Women's Chamber on TV too. When do they want to come?"

The interview proceeded smoothly, and to my surprise, my phone started ringing shortly afterward, a rarity for TV appearances, which are typically solely a branding opportunity, only yielding results much later. My belief is that this unique and timely exposure was especially impactful because thirty years ago, in Austin, dependable home-service businesses, staffed by individuals who could communicate in English, were still a scarce commodity. Most of the cleanings were still performed by individuals that the industry called trunk slammers. I unequivocally emphasized on the nightly news that my company only employed, and would continue to employ, documented cleaners proficient in English, a commitment that held true for all twenty-four of my employees at the time. The rest of the story will be revealed in a subsequent chapter.

As I mentioned earlier, during my time with the Austin Junior Forum, I had the privilege of being featured on television more than ten times. What stands out most vividly in my memory is my involvement in puppet shows, a unique and cherished experience. As previously mentioned, the Austin Junior Forum's core mission was to support women and children in need, and one of our outreach initiatives involved performing puppet shows for students ranging from kindergarten to fourth grade. These shows tackled challenging social issues of that era, including bullying, parental abuse, and the concept of "stranger danger."

Behind a draped table, we concealed ourselves, allowing only our puppets to be visible to the children in the audience. It was a remarkably enjoyable and rewarding endeavor because we genuinely made a positive impact on many young lives. After our performances, numerous students would approach their teachers and confide, "That happened to me." This heartfelt response was immensely gratifying for all of us.

These puppet shows served as a vital means of educating young children on sensitive topics, providing them with a safe space to discuss their concerns, a necessity, especially with today's social media platforms. Even now, creating such a comfortable venue for discussing these issues remains a challenge.

One of our TV appearances occurred unexpectedly when a parent contacted a local TV station to commend their school's participation in this program. The puppet show captured their attention, and we found ourselves on television once again. During the TV interview, they not only displayed my name but also the name of our company, a courtesy typically extended to business owners. This exposure to thousands of viewers, showcasing our community involvement, amounted to advertising and branding that would have cost a substantial sum if pursued through traditional means.

However, as the saying goes, "Every silver lining has its occasional rain cloud," and I encountered one such cloud during one of my TV appearances. The chamber approached me with a request to volunteer for mock employment interviews with prisoners, an idea aimed at potentially reducing recidivism by facilitating employment opportunities for former inmates. It was an intriguing proposition, considering I had never been incarcerated myself. I recognized that hiring individuals with a criminal record would likely be challenging, as my clients would understandably have reservations about welcoming a felon into their homes, especially for convictions like theft, child abuse, or assault.

Nonetheless, I volunteered for this project out of pure philanthropic intent, believing that these individuals deserved a chance and, perhaps, I could make a positive impact on their lives. I felt fortunate to have been raised by parents who instilled values and principles in me, enabling me to lead a successful and lawful life. The journey to the prison for the mock interviews was an hour-and-a-half drive, but it proved to be an enlightening experience. We passed through the gates, underwent security checks, and then settled at tables. Prisoners had the opportunity to select the profession they wanted to practice interviewing for. It was gratifying to witness their engagement and eagerness to improve their interviewing skills, along with their insightful questions on how to enhance their chances as job candidates. I provided honest feedback when they asked if I would hire them and recommended alternative employment options that aligned with their backgrounds.

Unexpectedly, during the interviews, an Austin television station arrived. This unforeseen development transformed my philanthropic endeavor into, what we thought, was a major success story for our company. While major corporations like Motorola, 3M, and Texas Instruments were also present, it was unusual to see someone from the cleaning industry, especially back in 1992, participating in such events. I was interviewed because it piqued the station's interest, a home-service business making a difference in the community.

When the story aired that same evening, I received phone calls from viewers who had watched the interview and congratulated me on my commitment to community service. The following morning, I received another call from a lady who had seen the interview and wanted to discuss it. This encounter underscored how my volunteering efforts and the long drive had unexpectedly turned into a valuable opportunity. However, her reaction was far from positive.

"Ms. Butza, I saw you on the news last night," she said, her voice tight.

"Oh, thank you for watching," I replied warmly.

"I won't be using your services anymore."

I was stunned. "I'm sorry to hear that. May I ask why?"

"You're involved with prisoners. I can't have someone cleaning my home who works with criminals."

"Ma'am, I was volunteering to help them practice job interviews. None of our cleaning staff has a criminal record. I would never—"

"I don't care," she interrupted. "I just can't support it."

I took a breath. "I understand. However, I want you to know that if you change your mind, we won't be able to provide services to your home."

There was a pause. "Excuse me?"

"With all due respect, our company values include community service and giving people second chances. If you can't support that, then we're probably not the right fit for each other."

She hung up.

I was astonished by her response, grateful that we did not need such a customer and grateful there weren't Google reviews yet.

This incident left me reflecting on the value of integrity and how it can sometimes be questioned, especially when financial considerations are involved. While money can enhance integrity, it can also erode it when the pursuit of wealth takes precedence over ethical principles.

One ongoing source of television exposure that is still a benefit available to cleaning services today is Cleaning for a Reason. I had the opportunity to be featured on TV five times through this organization. While I actively sought coverage the first four times, the fifth time, they reached out to me. Prior to Cancer Awareness

Month, I sent press releases to every local television station, radio station, and magazine, highlighting my involvement in Cleaning for a Reason and the free cleaning services offered to female cancer patients.

Participation in this organization is highly recommended for residential cleaning services. Today, membership requirements typically include cleaning the homes of at least two cancer patients twice in a year, a total of four cleanings. Cleaning for a Reason is affiliated with ISSA.com, the world's largest cleaning service organization, encompassing both commercial and residential cleaning services. In my press release, I emphasized the organization's national scope and elaborated on the assistance we provided to cancer patients. I even offered to arrange for a cancer patient whose home could serve as a convenient location for a TV spot, understanding that media interviewers often seek the path of least resistance. As a result, I was featured on three different television stations, which coincided perfectly with our company's growth during the back-to-school season.

The experience was not only rewarding for the cleaning team featured on TV but also for the cancer patient who agreed to participate. The requests for cleanings were coordinated through ISSA, ensuring that deserving cancer patients received the assistance they needed. Although cleaners were compensated for their time, the sense of fulfillment they derived from this charitable act was immeasurable. Interestingly, the morale of the entire company received a boost when one of our teams appeared on television. Even those who were not part of the TV appearance proudly proclaimed, "That's my company."

Television advertising of this nature incurs no direct costs beyond the time invested in gathering contact information for TV and radio stations, magazines, and newspapers. Initially, none of these media outlets reached out to me after sending the press releases. I secured TV coverage by following up with phone calls. While it does require some effort, I managed to get on three television stations in the first year. Although my success diminished in subsequent years, it is advisable to pursue this avenue consistently every year. When there's little else happening in the news cycle, there's a good chance that you'll be interviewed on at least one station.

One of the most valuable lessons I carried with me from the corporate world was the power of repetitive exposure. Early in my career, we were taught that a person needs to see your name at least seventeen times before they feel comfortable picking up the phone and asking for a quote. Today, depending on the research, that number ranges anywhere from seven to seventeen. I would be shocked if it were any lower. If anything, the noise of modern life probably demands more repetition, not less.

With that number in mind, every marketing decision I made was intentional. I wasn't interested in being seen once by a few people. I wanted to be seen once by a lot of people. One appearance on local television reached forty thousand viewers. That knocked off one of those required impressions instantly, compared to a mailing that might reach a hundred homes. The same logic applied to charity events and auctions. After my first decade in business, I stopped donating free cleanings unless there were at least a hundred people in the room. If a gala had a thousand attendees, that meant a thousand people had now seen my company name once. I only needed to find sixteen more places they might encounter it. Repetition builds familiarity. Familiarity builds trust. And trust is what makes the phone ring.

That strategy worked. The phone rang more often. The calendar filled faster. And with every new client we gained, the real pressure shifted inward, from getting noticed to delivering consistently. Growth doesn't just test marketing; it exposes operations, systems, and people. As the business expanded, the challenges stopped being about visibility and started being about what happens behind the scenes. And that's when I learned that not every problem announces itself honestly.

CHAPTER 6

THE COST OF STABILITY

After two years in the cleaning business, the results of my early decisions were finally starting to show. The constant work I had put into hiring, training, and retaining entry-level employees was paying off, slowly, imperfectly, but unmistakably. I had immersed myself in learning the residential cleaning industry, studying everything I could get my hands on. I didn't keep that knowledge to myself. I shared it with my cleaners, refining how we worked, how fast we cleaned, and how consistently we delivered results. Those systems worked. And almost without realizing it, we grew to ten cleaners.

That growth exposed a problem I hadn't anticipated: where the business actually lived. As the company found its footing, the work itself wasn't the only thing evolving. Our physical space, where we interviewed, dispatched teams, stored supplies, and washed endless mountains of towels, suddenly mattered far more than it had when we were small. In theory, clients never came to our office. Occasionally someone stopped by to drop off a key or a check, but otherwise, the business existed inside their homes, not ours. So I assumed where *we* worked didn't matter. In reality, it mattered a great deal—legally, operationally, and personally.

We had started in our tiny 1,150-square-foot, three-bedroom, one-and-a-half-bath home. The bedrooms were so small I'm not entirely sure "bedroom" was the right word, but I turned one of them into my office. That's where I interviewed, answered phones, and ran the business. Interviewing out of a back bedroom has its pros and cons.

Pro: a short commute.

Con: it looks exactly like what it was, a small start-up running on hope and caffeine.

What I hadn't fully understood at the time was that we were never properly zoned to operate a commercial business out of a residential home. Back then, working from home was almost unheard of. This was long before remote work became normal. Maybe one person in ten thousand ran a business out of their house. Neighbors didn't allow it, and cities certainly didn't license it. If we were small, no one noticed. But once ten cleaners started showing up every morning, parking throughout the cul-de-sac, the business became visible; and visibility changes everything.

That was when I learned an important lesson: Growth doesn't just stretch your systems. It tests your space, your neighbors, and the rules you didn't even know applied to you

Back then, employees did not feel confident working for start-ups. Everyone wanted the safety of the big blue companies. IBM was still the gold standard and the dream job. So bringing someone into my cramped little bedroom to interview them was, well, let's just say it wasn't the best recruiting tool.

To distract from the decor, I showed candidates a very sophisticated organizational chart I had borrowed from my MCI days. It had spaces for sixty employees, and I plugged our five names in as if we were halfway there already. For whatever reason, this entry-level crowd was blown away by an org chart. I'm convinced most had never seen one before. I do believe that simple little org chart was the reason I was able to recruit cleaners out of a bedroom. But that wasn't the main reason we needed to move.

Networking with real estate agents at chamber events brought me the knowledge that we were not supposed to be running a business out of our home. Therefore, ten cleaners coming to our home every morning, circling our cul-de-sac, parking anywhere they could and then driving off at a hurried speed was not sitting well with the neighbors. They weren't thrilled with our "daily parade," but the real breaking point came the day my less-than-tactful husband got into an argument with one of our cleaners. She drove off, rolled down her window, screamed words I will not repeat here, and punctuated her exit by waving her middle finger proudly out the window as she drove away. That was the moment I knew: It was time to move.

I don't know if any neighbors saw it (they all worked during the day),but I wasn't going to wait to find out. The writing was on the wall, and it was written in all caps.

A week earlier, while grocery shopping, I noticed a small warehouse office complex advertising, "First Month Free." That was all I needed to see. I sent my husband over to sign the lease and figured I'd worry about the second month later. It was cheap, it was scrappy, and, best of all, it was filled with other struggling start-ups. Window washers, builders, carpet cleaners…we fit right in. And they loved my dog.

Higgins, our well-trained English cocker spaniel, was another decision we had to make when we moved from our home into an office. What happens to a very spoiled but exceptionally well-behaved dog when the business outgrows the house? Because we didn't have children, Higgins was our child. I got him shortly after leaving my job at MCI. I remember saying that if I was going to walk away from a high-paying, cushy corporate position, the one privilege I deserved was to finally have a dog. The corporate world had never allowed it. I would have gone too many hours a day to do it responsibly.

There was more to it than that. At the time, Mike and I were already struggling in our marriage. We were working nonstop, twenty-four hours a day, seven days a week, and had started seeing a marriage counselor. One of the best pieces of advice she gave us, especially for couples running a business together, was to find something outside the business that we could share. Her suggestion was simple: to get a dog. We wanted one anyway, so we scraped together the money for a purebred English Cocker, and along came Higgins.

He turned out to be a wonderful diversion. I trained him for twenty minutes every morning and every night for ninety days, and it showed. He was exceptionally well behaved. Wherever we went, Higgins went with us. If we flew home for the holidays, Higgins flew home too. So, when we moved into the warehouse office, the question became obvious: Did Higgins come with us?

Back then, bringing a dog to the office was unheard of. This was long before dogs in workplaces were normalized. It wasn't considered professional. But the office was part warehouse, part dispatch center, and Higgins came with us. The cleaners loved him. He didn't jump on them or bark or demand attention. He simply sat near the door, wagging his tail, quietly hoping someone would stop and pet him. He had a calming presence, and people smiled the moment they walked in.

Over time, I realized that bringing Higgins to the office was one of the smartest decisions I ever made. When applicants came in to apply for a job, Higgins became an unintentional screening tool. If someone recoiled at the sight of a calm, well-trained dog sitting politely at the door, I knew immediately they weren't cut out to work inside people's homes. This was the period when dogs were becoming part of the family, not just pets. Most of our clients had dogs they loved like children, and cleaners needed to be comfortable around them.

Higgins did more than keep us company. He softened the office; lowered stress; and gave me insight into the people I was hiring, before they ever picked up a towel.

The warehouse became our new headquarters. We washed and dried towels there, kept supplies, and did morning dispatch. There was even a small office that looked slightly more sophisticated than my back-bedroom setup. At least when I interviewed candidates there, they no longer felt like they were entering a witness-protection safehouse.

We stayed in that location for about two years and grew a lot. We also washed a mountain of towels back then, pre-microfiber days, which ultimately became the reason we had to move again. But that's a story for a later chapter.

Once we were settled in that second office, other business challenges started to reveal themselves—some expected, some not at all. And one of those unexpected challenges walked right into my office one day in the form of Susan Martinez.

A significant portion of my workforce consisted of welfare recipients who perceived an opportunity to augment their income by working for me, effectively supplementing their welfare checks. While technically permissible, earning more than an extra $50 per week presented a dilemma. If they earned more, their welfare benefits would decrease. It was a tricky balance. To address this challenge, I devised a system, which I'll discuss later, that would make working with me financially appealing for these individuals.

Among my dedicated employees, Susan Martinez stood out as one of the brightest stars. She was a married woman, the primary breadwinner for her husband and their three wonderful children. Susan approached her job with unwavering commitment, and her cleaning skills were truly exceptional. In times of need, she often saved the day by taking on extra cleaning assignments when other employees called in sick.

One day, Susan walked into my office with a concerning predicament. She knocked tentatively on the door frame.

"Sharon, do you have a minute?"

"Of course, Susan. Come in, sit down."

She perched on the edge of the chair, wringing her hands. "My car broke down. The transmission went out."

"Oh no, I'm sorry to hear that."

"I'm using my husband's vehicle today, but it's only available today. He needs it for work tomorrow." She paused, then looked me directly in the eyes. "Unless you pay for a new transmission for my car, I'm going to have to quit."

I stared at her, processing what I'd just heard. Then I said firmly, "That's blackmail, Susan."

To my astonishment, she simply nodded. "I know."

I realized that if I gave in and paid for the transmission, there was no guarantee she would remain in her position, and I would be stuck with a hefty repair bill. Pragmatic as I was, I ran a business, not a charity. Consequently, I decided to take matters into my own hands.

Without delay, I had my husband purchase five cars the following day, ensuring that he didn't spend more than $500 on any of them. I deliberately avoided branding these vehicles with the company name since they weren't exactly a testament to our professionalism. During those times, we refrained from adding any company decals, hoping that potential clients wouldn't recognize them as our company cars. One of the vehicles was bright yellow and resembled a taxicab, an amusing coincidence given today's trends where such a color might actually be desirable for a company vehicle. Although there was no need to worry about my employees using these vehicles for personal purposes. They could not wait to get them home and park them. My objective became to phase them out as swiftly as possible.

However, providing company cars resolved my supervisor turnover issues. I did not need another supervisor for the next nine months and that was due to growth. Prior to introducing company vehicles, anyone with a car and a driver's license could secure a job one day, quit the next, return the next; and I would hire them again as a supervisor. The scarcity of drivers with vehicles was a dire concern. Company cars fixed that problem, so eventually, I decided to part ways with the old cars by sending them to the junkyard and investing in five nearly new GEO Metros. One of the vehicles had accumulated fewer than ten thousand miles and set me back just under $10,000.

The memory of preparing for the loan to acquire those cars remains etched in my mind. I turned to the financial book my VP at MCI had given me and methodically organized my paperwork into a leather-bound portfolio, not because I believed presentation would change the decision but because preparation mattered to me. Being organized didn't guarantee approval, and being a woman didn't give you extra points. Banks still lent money based on comfort, not just numbers.

My appointment with Kevin, the branch manager at Chase Bank, was arranged quickly thanks to our connection through the chamber board. He reviewed my paperwork for no more than five minutes before leaning back in his chair and asking the question that told me exactly where this conversation was headed.

"Sharon," he said, "do you genuinely believe people are going to give you a key to their house?"

I leaned forward. "Kevin, many of our clients prefer it. The peace of mind they get from coming home to a clean house outweighs the concern. We're bonded, insured, and we do background checks."

He wasn't convinced.

"I'll tell you what," he said. "You give me fifty thousand dollars to put into a CD, and I'll approve a fifty-thousand-dollar loan."

My answer was immediate. "Kevin, I'm not that naïve. I'm not giving you fifty thousand dollars so you can loan it back to me with interest.

He shifted in his seat. Kevin could see my accounts. He knew I had the money. What he didn't understand was that I had no intention of using my own savings to satisfy his discomfort with my business model. I walked out of that office, went back to the dealership, and secured better terms through GMAC Financing.

At the time, I chalked it up to another reminder of how slowly women were moving forward in the financial world. It echoed the story about the founders of the Austin Junior Forum with ideas that didn't fit the mold. Women had and still have a long ways to go before there is an equal playing field with men.

What makes the story complete, though, is what happened later.

About a year after that meeting, Kevin became a client.

I suspect his wife insisted. Kevin could never remember to leave a key, and he was last to leave the house. We'd arrive at the house and have to leave, unable to clean. It happened more than once.

Finally, one day, I told him plainly, "Kevin, if you don't give us a key, we're not cleaning your house anymore."

That afternoon, he showed up at the office, key in hand. As he handed it to me, we both started laughing.

"Well," I said, smiling, "it turns out people will give you a key to their house."

He returned my smile.

I had the distinct feeling he was in serious trouble at home that day and needed that house cleaned, immediately. Whatever conversation had happened between Kevin and his wife, I suspect it was far more uncomfortable than our loan meeting had ever been. He ate a little crow from two women that afternoon, and we both knew it.

The irony wasn't lost on me. The very thing he couldn't believe would ever work became the reason he became a client. And that, more than any rebuttal I could have offered in his office, proved the point.

The new cars were handed over to our five supervisors, who were ecstatic about the prospect. However, just two weeks later, I was shocked to discover that each car had already incurred some form of damage. Some had cigarette burns in the front seats, others had stains in the back, and a few were even filled with garbage. I couldn't contain my frustration and delivered a stern message.

I called an emergency meeting and stood before all five supervisors. Something that, you will learn in future chapters, is against everything I stand for as a leader. I was so irritated I could not control my emotions.

"I cannot believe what I'm seeing," I began, my voice tight with controlled anger. "These were nearly brand-new cars. Two weeks ago, they were spotless. Now every single one has cigarette burns, stains, or trash everywhere."

The supervisors looked at the floor, at each other, anywhere but at me.

"Let me be very clear," I continued. "None of you will ever receive a like-new car from me again. Ever."

I remained true to my word, and from that point onward, I only purchased very old, used cars. Nonetheless, the employees valued having access to transportation, as many of them would not have been able to work without a vehicle. This was especially significant for those who relied on someone to pick them up from their homes en route to their first job location.

I firmly advocate the use of company vehicles, particularly when building a business with a focus on repeat clients. I believe that the primary reason for cancellations among repeat clients is "too many different faces in my home." If your business relies heavily on one-time visits, employee turnover may not be as critical as it is when the majority of your business comes from repeat clients. Furthermore, I would submit that the leading cause of employee turnover is transportation issues when you do not provide company transportation.

Company vehicles can also significantly ease the recruitment process. Over the years, I've been involved in recruiting efforts, both as a business owner and as part of my consulting services. I have a steadfast rule: I will not recruit for a company that does not offer company vehicles. Asking potential candidates about their possession of a valid driver's license and dependable transportation is often the first question, and it usually eliminates half of the candidates immediately. This is particularly problematic when only a small fraction of the eligible population is actively seeking employment, much less cleaning employment.

Company vehicles play a pivotal role in enhancing brand visibility and serve as moving advertisements, especially within gated communities. It's remarkable to note that an impressive 30 percent of our total sales were directly attributed to the presence of our company vehicles. If you're currently operating a home-service business, I strongly urge you to consider this question: "Do you have a clear understanding of the cost associated with acquiring a repeat client?" Unfortunately, many business owners lack this crucial insight. For those who do, estimates often fall in the range of \$175 to \$280 per repeat client, undoubtedly a significant investment.

Surprisingly, the cost of acquiring a company vehicle can sometimes rival or even fall below this range. In certain cases, it may even prove to be more cost-effective than the expenses associated with acquiring and retaining repeat clients. The tangible benefits of having company vehicles extend beyond mere transportation. They have a profoundly positive impact on your bottom line by reducing employee turnover among your cleaning staff, subsequently leading to a reduction in repeat client turnover. In today's fiercely competitive job market, especially if you aspire to maintain a clientele of 100 percent repeat customers while achieving annual revenues exceeding \$3 million, company vehicles can be considered almost indispensable.

It is a proven fact that a company will gross \$25 to \$30K more per cleaner per year when the cleaner operates as a solo, and expenses are drastically reduced when a solo drives their own vehicle. That financial reality cannot be ignored and deserves to be acknowledged. Solos are profitable on paper, and for many owners, that math is extremely compelling.

Unfortunately, that higher profitability often comes at a hidden cost, cleaner attrition and client attrition, which in many cases becomes a bigger issue than the lost revenue when using teams. Solos put far more wear and tear on their own vehicles, absorb the cost of breakdowns, and spend long hours alone inside homes. It is isolating work, and over time, that isolation contributes to burnout. While a company may not be able to afford to provide company cars to solo cleaners, asking cleaners to continually sacrifice their own vehicles and work in isolation is rarely sustainable long term.

I do not have statistics tracking the financial impact of lowering employee and client turnover or the long-term value of the advertising and branding gained per company vehicle. What I do know, based on real-world experience, is that several large companies moved away from teams and company vehicles during the COVID period in favor of solos, only to reverse course later.

The reason wasn't financial. It was operational. Client complaints increased, particularly around unfamiliar faces in the home, and cleaner turnover continued to climb. Many of those companies ultimately returned to teams and company vehicles, along with solos driving their own cars, not because they were cheaper but because they were more stable.

What those decisions also brought with them, however, was a new layer of complexity. Teams require coordination. Company vehicles require oversight. Supplies, laundry, scheduling, storage, accountability, and space all expand as soon as you move beyond survival mode. Stability solved one set of problems, but it introduced another. Growth no longer hinged on getting clients or keeping cleaners. It hinged on managing details well enough that the entire operation didn't buckle under its own weight.

That was the point where the business truly changed.

CHAPTER 7

GROWTH REQUIRES EMPLOYEES

In my fifty-one years of business experience, one consistent factor among business owners who have grown multimillion-dollar companies is their ability to find and retain employees. Regardless of the industry, there is usually a pool of potential workers available if you are willing to do what it takes to recruit and keep them.

Leaving my high-paying corporate job in 1988 and joining the company wasn't an ideal time, as Texas was undergoing a major recession. However, this challenge did not negatively impact our start-up company. In fact, I often say that recessions can be beneficial, as they weed out companies that shouldn't have been in business in the first place. Poorly organized companies with subpar customer service and low-quality cleanings harm our industry. When the economy is strong, these companies can survive, but during recessions, only the best remain. Satisfied customers benefit the entire industry by spreading positive word of mouth.

We were fortunate to be in Austin, Texas, in 1988 when the recession hit. Although it affected builders and oil and gas owners, our diversified economy helped us. High-tech companies like Motorola and AMD were moving to Austin, transforming it into what was being called Silicon Hills. By the early nineties, Austin was booming.

However, this boom presented challenges in recruiting new cleaners. Margins in our industry are tight, so we couldn't offer high salaries. In the late eighties, customers were still unwilling to pay much for cleaning services. We charged $39.95 plus taxes to clean a small home, which left little room to pay our employees well. Initially, I started Keri at minimum wage, plus a small bonus for driving. It was difficult to compete for employees against corporations offering benefits. Yet we were also blessed with an influx of customers, allowing us to gradually raise salaries and offer bonuses and benefits.

One unique benefit we offered was company cars for supervisors, which they could take home and use to pick up and drop off their partners each day. This perk significantly helped with recruitment and retention. Our brand recognition in Austin, a city of about 250,000 people at the time, was strong, further aiding our recruiting efforts. We developed a reputation for fairness, good pay, and company vehicles, making us an attractive employer.

I brought Colleen on board as a partner for Susan. If you recall, Susan was an excellent cleaner. What she was not is an excellent supervisor. She had absolutely no managerial finesse or any desire to gain any. It's possible that she would have been better off working independently, but her lack of a reliable vehicle made that impractical. Providing company vehicles to solo cleaners was not financially feasible due to tight margins.

Recruiting cleaners for the company has never been easy, and it remains a challenging task even after thirty-six years in the business. Susan's tendency to drive away her partners presented a unique challenge. She was incredibly punctual and dedicated; but if a partner she finally liked had to miss a day of work after ninety days, she would change her attitude toward them, becoming dictatorial and difficult to work with. Cleaning may not be inherently fun, but it's the camaraderie with colleagues that can make it enjoyable, just as in any other profession.

Colleen was hired on the day before her first workday. She had prior experience and was actually impressive with her tall, thin, and commanding presence, paired with a distinctive Southern drawl. Colleen had a son, a daughter, and a less-than-helpful husband; but at least he didn't treat her as badly as Susan's husband treated her. Neither of them had what one would call a functional family.

Colleen showed up promptly on her first day, ready to work. I introduced her to Susan, and they prepared their supplies and headed out to work together. I fervently hoped that the two of them would get along, and Colleen would live up to her promises.

With a fully staffed team, I didn't waste any time catching up on tasks that had been neglected during Colleen's recruitment. Keri and I took a rare break for lunch, savoring our favorite Sonic salad. Lunch breaks were a luxury we seldom enjoyed unless it was a business luncheon.

I returned to my office, but soon enough, Colleen surprised me by appearing at my doorway.

"What do you want me to do next?" she asked. "My husband won't be here for another four hours."

I was taken aback by her presence. "Colleen? What are you doing here? Where's Susan?"

Colleen shrugged. "We had an argument after the first job, and Susan stopped the car on I-35 and made me get out. I walked back here."

I was stunned. "She dropped you off on the freeway? And you walked back?"

"Yes, ma'am. It took me about an hour."

I don't even remember the reason for their argument, but I couldn't fathom the idea of someone walking back to the office after such an incident. I promoted Colleen to a supervisor position on the spot. She agreed to wait a couple of days before starting, giving me time to purchase a car for her. I sent Mike to find another car and hired two new partners, one for Colleen and one for Susan. This was a significant opportunity for growth, and I had to add another team to meet my annual goals.

Colleen worked for me for eighteen years, with only one three-month absence, which I will discuss in a later chapter, and never missed a day. She was bright, fast, reliable, and consistent.

Over those years, she moved from a team of two to a team of three, changing partners only three times. Tragically, one partner passed away.

In her last decade with the company, her partners often didn't speak English at first. Colleen didn't mind. Neither did they. They learned enough over time, and under Colleen's leadership, they had perfect attendance.

They slept in like many young people do. Colleen handled that too. We had company cars, and she'd pick them up on the way to work. If they weren't at the door when she arrived, she honked once, waited, then walked inside, went to their bedroom, and literally pulled them out of bed.

"You're coming to work today because I ain't workin' with nobody else," she'd say in that Southern drawl. "Get up and get dressed. I'm waitin' in the car."

And they would. They loved her. She was like a mother to them.

They finished early, made good money, and clients adored them because they had the same cleaners year after year. They received generous Christmas tips, two thousand dollars each, and the cleaners were profoundly grateful. They were simply delightful people to work with.

Colleen would, ultimately, end up being one of the most influential employees we ever hired. She was often the catalyst for growth in our company because of positive or negative conduct. I still often think of Colleen when I see a Dell laptop.

Michael Dell, also an Austin native, founded his company with just $1,000 in 1986, a perfect time to start a tech venture. We had the privilege of cleaning the home of one of his initial "seed money" backers as his enterprise began to flourish. By 1996, Dell had entered the private sector laptop market; and the rest, as they say, is history. Attracted by a significant tax incentive from the city of Austin, Dell Computers established its roots and expanded its operations in the city. Dell built factories and set up his corporate headquarters in Austin, bringing in a wealth of talented and high-income professionals.

However, despite the influx of skilled workers, he faced a significant challenge: staffing his numerous factories. Austin, brimming with college students, was not ideal for recruiting factory workers. As I mentioned earlier, while Austin was perfect for high-tech offices like MCI Long Distance, it wasn't conducive to attracting entry-level employees. Michael Dell experienced this firsthand. His factory workers started at minimum wage, just like ours. Realizing this wage wouldn't suffice to meet the growing demand for his laptops in 1996, he turned to temporary agencies. He offered three dollars an hour above minimum wage, with the promise of health-care benefits in ninety days. This move created a severe backlash for small-business owners like us, as temporary agencies capitalized on these lucrative offers, swiftly depleting the available workforce and leaving us struggling to compete.

Temporary agencies stood to make a mint of money. All they needed to do was advertise their hourly rate with future benefits, and they could wipe out the average service industry owner of most of their employees in less than a week.

I will never forget the devastating day when disaster struck our company. I arrived at the office early for a Chamber meeting, only to find Keri already pulling into the driveway. However, something unusual greeted both of us: One of our company vehicles was inexplicably parked there. With a fleet of about fourteen vehicles, we had stopped recognizing each one on sight.

We rushed into the office to check the messages, but there were none. We pulled the license plate list and realized it was Colleen's car. This was highly unusual and unlike Colleen. I tried calling her, but there was no answer. Meanwhile, Keri had been conducting her own investigation. She came into my office with an alarming discovery.

"Sharon, look at this," Keri said, holding up a set of keys. "Colleen's keys, files, pager, car keys, everything that belongs to the company—all left inside the locked car."

"What? That doesn't make any sense."

"I had to use the spare keys to open it."

This unsettling revelation deepened the mystery and heightened our concern.

We spent the next hour redistributing Colleen's assignments and ensuring our other teams could cover her jobs. Unfortunately, her partner was also unreachable, leaving us short-staffed by two. Colleen handled numerous regular clients daily, so we had to inform each one that a different team would be cleaning their home. We hoped some might skip their cleaning for the day, but no such luck.

Although Colleen's departure on a Monday, a typically slow day for residential cleaning services, would seem fortunate, we had successfully learned how to fill our Monday schedule over the years; so every day was busy. We immediately called in our two relief staff members, but we were still short a supervisor. To manage, I split up another team with two drivers, convincing the second driver to supervise and drive for the day. I paired each relief person with one of them and reassigned some jobs to teams eager for overtime. By the end of the hour, we had a plan in place for the day. Keri would handle the rest of the week and continue searching for Colleen and her partner. With the immediate crisis managed, I headed off to my chamber meeting.

Ironically, the topic dominating the chamber meeting before, during, and after was the acute employee shortage in Austin. The city's unemployment rate had plummeted to a mere 2.1%. Just a year earlier, it had been closer to the national average of 5.7%. Traditionally, Austin had a robust labor pool, bolstered by UT graduates who often chose to remain in the city postgraduation. The city's slow but steady growth usually ensured a steady stream of job openings for these new graduates.

Now, however, with unemployment at 2.1%, the situation was dire. More than 2.1% of Austin residents were retired, disabled, or incarcerated. Small businesses across every industry were struggling to find employees. While Michael Dell's influence had undeniably fueled Austin's boom, it also created a concurrent problem: an overwhelming demand for products and services, but a severe shortage of employees to fulfill those orders. Suddenly, every business faced the challenge of meeting customer needs with an insufficient workforce.

Keri and I spent the entire day trying to contact Colleen. Finally, around 4:30 p.m., we received a call from her.

"Sharon, it's Colleen," her voice was quiet, almost ashamed.

"Colleen! Where have you been? We've been so worried!"

"I'm so sorry. I felt embarrassed and didn't want to call you sooner."

"Embarrassed? About what?"

There was a pause. "I accepted a position at a temp agency. To work for Dell Computers."

My heart sank. "Oh."

"After everything you've done for me, I know this looks bad. I just…the money was better, and they're offering health-care benefits."

I couldn't blame her, but I also couldn't match her new job's offer of an extra dollar per hour and health-care benefits. Offering those benefits to Colleen would mean extending them to all employees, something our margins simply couldn't support. I had always operated like a corporation, treating everyone equally. Having previously defended EEOC charges in court, with MCI covering the attorney fees, I had no desire to face such challenges again. Matching Colleen's new salary and benefits was beyond our financial capacity.

In hindsight, perhaps our clients would have accepted a rate increase to keep Colleen, but not all of them would have been willing. Not every cleaner was a Colleen. At least, we finally knew what had happened. I set out to find a new relief cleaner and supervisor. The silver lining was that one of our current relief cleaners would likely move into a full-time position, offering a bit of good news amidst the day's challenges.

Anyone who contacted our company, regardless of whether we needed employees at the time, was asked for their name, previous experience, driver's license status, proficiency in English and Spanish, and how they heard about us. I meticulously tracked this information in a three-ring binder that, by the time I left the company, had expanded to a massive four-inch ring binder. Depending on our level of desperation, we would search as far back in that binder as necessary to find a suitable cleaner.

Remember, this was before the era of online immediate gratification. We couldn't afford to wait for our ad to run in the classifieds and for the newspapers to be delivered to find candidates for urgently needed positions. While we did run ads, we typically filled our open positions from our binder, our "treasure chest," before any new calls came in. We continually added new names to this treasure chest.

Having a well-maintained treasure chest of potential candidates is crucial, especially today. Whether you're using platforms like Indeed, Woot Recruit, Hire-Chill-Lead, ZipRecruiter, or other third-party services, it's vital to take detailed notes on each candidate and mark them as hired if applicable. As your company grows, the number of people you have hired, terminated, or who have quit over the years will increase; and it's easy to forget those who were only with you for a short period.

In one desperate "I need a cleaner yesterday" moment, I mistakenly contacted someone from our treasure chest who had already been hired and fired by our company. She had only been with us for two days, so I didn't remember her, but she certainly remembered me. When I called her house to see if she was interested in returning, she curtly replied, "You already hired and fired me."

Yikes. This experience underscored the importance of paying meticulous attention to detail.

I made numerous phone calls from my treasure chest of candidates, but either no one answered or they were no longer interested. Most likely, they were starting at Dell the next day, earning far more than I could offer. I left a multitude of voice messages, hoping that at least one would call me back.

That evening, feeling deeply distraught and with no potential supervisor in sight, I prayed fervently all the way home. My concern for the future was well-founded, and I couldn't help but worry about what lay ahead.

With so much on our plates, Keri and I agreed to head to the office a bit earlier the next morning. We both arrived at 5:30 a.m., only to be met with another surprise: a car parked in the driveway. This time we immediately inspected the car and discovered it was the continuation of the serial exodus. Just like Colleen, everything was left inside.

"Not again," Keri breathed.

"Who is it this time?" I asked, already dreading the answer.

Keri checked the license plate against our list. "It's Beverly's team."

"Both of them?"

"Looks like it."

Realizing we had another team that wouldn't be showing up, not just for that day but likely indefinitely, we quickly set about reorganizing the day's schedule. I managed to persuade the two partners who were drivers to step up and take on long-term supervisory roles, which was a significant help. However, this meant I now needed to find two new partners and yet another supervisor to fill the gaps.

I did find one new hire, thanks to one of my loyal cleaners who brought their friend. I hired her on the spot, and she would be in a full-time position and fully trained by the next morning. We had to do a lot of shuffling to figure out how to get the houses cleaned on Wednesday, but miraculously, we were able to get everyone moved and covered. We both left that day confident. Even though we had lost another team, having done something once made doing it the second time much easier.

On the third day, as usual, Keri and I agreed to meet at 5:30 a.m., hoping for the best. To our dismay, but not surprise, we found yet another car parked in the driveway. I don't know how we managed not to burst into tears. Perhaps we simply didn't have the time.

Keri swiftly ran inside to grab the spare key, retrieved the keys and files from the car, and we hurried off to our offices to devise a plan for the day. With no other options available, I assigned eight jobs to Susan to handle solo. She completed them all. I doubt that she even bothered to bring in anything more than a feather duster, disinfectant cleaner, and one towel. Ironically, the only phone call I received from those eight homes was a client asking to have the same team back again. That was actually a scary thought for me. What did that house look like before Susan got there? I took a team of five myself and hoped for some skips.

All in all, I was relatively useless help. I would try and clean one thing while the five cleaners scurried around the house and cleaned everything else. I was very lucky if I could get the refrigerator cleaned by the time they were ready to go. Sometimes all I did was take their supplies out to the car when they were done using it.

I am sure if the police had stopped us, we would have received a ticket and had to remove one person from the car. We were driving those little GEO Metros with six people in them, four in the back seat and two in the front, along with supplies for five cleaners for the day in the hatchback. Some of the cleaners were holding mini-vacuum cleaners. At least if we had an accident, nobody would have flown around the car. A fly would've had difficulties getting in.

The cleaners were in a relatively good mood because this truly was an adventure for them and the "boss" was driving them around. Every time we arrived at a home that normally gave us access by hiding a key under the mat, we prayed that it wouldn't be there so we could get rid of another job. If they forgot the key, it would be impossible to clean the home. On a normal day, we would call the client and go pick up the key at their place of work. We would not want to lose the job and the revenue. Not this nightmare day when all we wanted was for the day to end.

Of course, we were not that fortunate. We made it through our jobs and got back to the office about six thirty that evening.

As soon as we got done figuring out how to get all the partners home and all the cleaners left the office, Keri broke down in tears.

She was used to a smooth-running operation where ninety-eight out of one hundred calls were compliments, scheduling, and sales. Now, suddenly, she had spent the entire day fielding complaints about different teams, wrong times, things cleaned differently, as well as responding to complaints about the change in times and teams for the following day.

We concluded that no matter what happens the next day I would not leave her alone in the office. Totally exhausted, we both went home and tried to get some sleep, agreeing to meet at five o'clock the next morning.

I am a believer that there are certain days in life that impact and change us forever. Thursday would become one of those days for me. It came as no surprise to Keri and me when we drove into the office driveway Thursday morning at five o'clock and saw another company car parked in the driveway. Number four supervisor exodus. Colleen truly had started a massacre. Another two people have mysteriously disappeared.

Some things had gotten easier. Any routine is easier than facing a situation for the first time. Driving in the driveway and seeing a company car sitting there, investigating who wouldn't be cleaning anymore and fixing the schedule accordingly had become routine. Keri would get the spare key, grab the keys and files out of the car, and return to her office to begin rearranging the day.

I would assist in this effort until the day was fixed and then go where needed. Keri had predecided the office is where I needed to be on this specific day. I believe this was the first and only time that Keri ever made any kind of a demand. I certainly didn't blame her. Yesterday had been brutal, and this day was going to be worse. Today we would need to inform Friday clients that they would not be cleaned the following day, right before the weekend.

At this time, my thoughts really weren't so much about how we were going to get through the day or even the week, my thoughts were about what we were going do for the next year, or even the rest of our lives, without this company. There were a lot of people dependent upon, and literally living off of, this company. For some of us, it was the only household income: Keri, some cleaners, Mike, and myself.

I never dreamed we would be at $1M gross income and I would still be thinking about the possibility of losing the company. I remember only too well how many times I was scared in the first two years of our start up that this company would never be able to support Mike and myself, much less another thirty employees. I thought those days were history, but they were not. I was feeling even more devastated today than I felt then.

Another one of my mother's favorite sayings was "Necessity is the mother of invention," and I know that is true. It is what got me through so many challenges in the past ten years. I couldn't just create a cleaner. If only I could purchase a robot. I literally had nowhere or anybody to turn to, to find a solution to the possible death of our company.

Again, this was 1996. Google search was not well-known, or well developed, until 2000 to 2004. Consequently, whenever challenges presented themselves, we had to make things up to fix the challenges. We did have goals and plans, but we did not have Google and Facebook to warn us of what was to come and provide us with downloads to put proactive preventative fixes in place.

When faced with new challenges, we tried different ideas until we found one that worked. I would submit that most new and innovative ideas have come from a simple, or difficult, need. I can still remember the clever ways my father managed to get the cows milked when the electricity went out. What a precarious situation he found himself in, over which he had no control, but the cows had to be milked. My situation was no different. The houses have to be cleaned, or I would simply be out of business. If we are not cleaning enough homes to cover payroll, minimal expenses, and our living costs, the result is very simple—we are out of business.

It took a considerable amount of time to get the day organized and get all of the cleaners picked up and at their first job. As soon as everything was in place, I focused 100 percent of my time and attention to trying to find more cleaners. It seemed like a dauntless effort: Everyone I called was already working at Dell computers.

In the middle of this tireless effort, my banker called and asked if I wanted to meet her for lunch. We had not seen each other since the chamber meeting, the first day of the mass exodus. She wanted to catch up.

"Sharon, it's Rhoda. Want to grab lunch today?"

"Rhoda, I can't. We're in the middle of a crisis. I might be going out of business."

"What? What happened?"

I quickly explained the nightmare of the past four days: the mass exodus, the abandoned cars, the desperate scrambling.

"Sharon, you have to meet me for lunch. I have an idea that might save your business."

I looked at Keri, who was on three phone lines at once trying to reschedule clients. "I don't know if I can leave,"

"One hour. That's all I'm asking. I really think I can help."

I sighed. "Okay. Where?"

"Our usual place. Noon."

I told Keri I was going to lunch to learn how to save our company. Keri knew and respected Rhoda and thought it was a very good idea because Keri was also desperate and could not think of anything to do to find cleaners.

Noon could not come fast enough for me. I was hopeful that Rhoda would give me the answer to my $64,000 question, Where do I find cleaners? But I never dreamed she would ultimately change our company forever. We met at our favorite restaurant, and both ordered tea and salads and got right down to talking business.

"Okay, tell me everything," Rhoda said, leaning forward.

I recounted the entire ordeal, Colleen's defection, the domino effect, the four teams gone in four days.

Rhoda listened intently, then said, "I think I know what you need to do, but you're not going to like it."

"At this point, I'll try anything."

"You need to do what John at The House Cleaners is doing—hire Hispanic cleaners."

I stared at her. "Rhoda, you know I can't do that. I went on television and told all of Austin that I would never have a cleaner in a home who couldn't speak English. What would that do to my integrity?"

Rhoda didn't flinch. She looked me straight in the eye and asked, "Is your integrity worth losing your company?"

The words hit me like a slap.

"Think about it," she continued. "What will your employees think about your integrity if they're out of a job, something you promised would never happen to them?"

I opened my mouth to argue, but nothing came out.

"John at The House Cleaners is growing faster than you are," Rhoda said. "He puts five people in a car. Four of them don't speak English. The driver is bilingual and manages the team. That's it. That's his model."

"But how does he communicate with them? How does he train them?"

"Figure it out, Sharon. You're smart. You always figure it out."

We finished lunch mostly in silence. I told her I'd think about it, but honestly, I thought it was a terrible idea.

I went back to the office and shared Rhoda's suggestion with Keri.

"Hispanic cleaners who don't speak English?" Keri's eyes widened. "How would we manage these people?"

"I don't know," I admitted. "I don't know either."

But I did pull out the huge stack of applications I had on my desk from Hispanics who had walked in the door wanting to work for our company. We offered more hours than any of our competitors, and we gave company cars to supervisors to take home and use to pick up and drop off their partners at their homes.

Somehow we made it through that day and rearranged Friday, but we hadn't started working on the next week at all. We decided they could wait until Friday when I figured out what I was going to do with this mess. We left the office at five thirty that night. We came to the conclusion that staying any longer wouldn't do us any good. The damage was done, and now we need to figure out how to recoup. We needed a night of thinking and working on the business and not working in it.

I decided it was time for me to go to an Al-Anon meeting. I needed some support from someone. I needed to get off my pity pot. At least, I needed to clear my head and start thinking rationally rather than emotionally.

I joined Al-Anon a couple years before when my alcoholic husband finally agreed to go to Alcoholics Anonymous. My heart went out to him because he was an only child of two alcoholic parents. Mike spent most of his life raising them rather than the opposite. On the other hand, I had come from very strong parents who could have a six pack of beer in the refrigerator for a year.

Al-Anon was filled with people who had their own set of problems, or they probably would not have married an alcoholic. I was no exception, but because of my great upbringing I was stronger than most people in that room. My father said he felt sorry for children of alcoholics because the only way they knew to solve a problem was to reach for a beer. That was the behavior they learned as a child. Believe me, that was not the behavior I learned.

Within two years, I was basically running the chapter I belonged to. There were no designated leaders, but there are always people who "run the show" or keep things going. Many of our members were what I would call switch hitters. They would spend some nights in the AA room and some nights in the Al-Anon room. Many of them were alcoholics themselves but felt their spouse was more addicted and drank more. They attended Al-Anon to learn how to deal with their alcoholic spouse. They really were dealing with two separate issues in their lives. I respected them for their commitment to finding peace. At this point in my life, I could relate to it.

One couple who attended those meetings seemed permanently stuck in what I came to think of as a pity pot. They dominated the room whenever it was their turn to speak, using that time to complain, something that technically wasn't allowed. I never once heard them talk about anything constructive or forward moving. Neither of them was working. There was no sense of ambition, no plan, no effort to change their situation. They had started a business and lost it. They tried again and lost that one too. By the time I met them, they were living off the state, resigned to their circumstances, and fully committed to staying there.

When I started sharing my story from the week with the group, most of the members said, "You'll come through this like you come through everything." They gave me Al-Anon support jargon and tried to make me feel better. One statement was made, however, that really did change my life; and it came from the two losers.

"You know," the woman said quietly, "losing our two businesses was the best thing that ever happened to us."

I looked at her skeptically.

"I'm serious," she continued. "You should feel blessed by this opportunity that God has given you to start all over again."

I got in my car on the way home and thought there is no way I am a loser like those two people and there's no way I'm thanking God for this opportunity to lose my business. It sucks. Perhaps there is a silver lining somewhere, but it is not losing my business.

I realized at that moment that I had to find a solution for recruiting because I am never going to lose my business because I am not a loser. I am a victor, not a victim, as Joel Osteen would say.

On Friday morning, when I arrived at my desk, I went directly to my stack of Hispanic applications looking for anyone who had lots of years of experience. I was also hoping to find someone who was bilingual, but I wasn't that lucky. I somehow managed to communicate in some way with four cleaners for interviews, and they all showed up.

Now that I've worked with the Hispanic community for thirty years, I realize that that is just who they are. Most of them do what they say they're going to do, and they do it on time. When I set up interviews with respondents to my classified ads, the majority of which were welfare recipients, I would set up eight interviews and be lucky if one showed up. A bit like the employee market today.

I hired all four, and Keri began to tackle rearranging the cleaning schedule for the following week.

I had enough cleaners, but I was still short of four driving supervisors. The easiest way to fix that was to go from two-person teams to three-person teams and give them two extra jobs as a team. We rearranged the schedule for the next week using the new parameters and were able to cover all our jobs.

Keri and I both left the office that day feeling a new surge of excitement and hope. There would be growing pains with these huge changes. The teams needed to accept three on a team and, in the beginning, the third not speaking any English, which would be a huge change. The clients needed to accept three people in their house, which would also be a huge change for them.

We called the clients for Monday and made them aware of the change. We were confronted with some resentment, but everyone said they would give it a try, and no one canceled their service.

Keri and I did not change our morning routine for 5:00 a.m. on the following Monday. Just in case. So, as usual, we arrived at the same time and drove into the driveway, but something was unusual. There was no company vehicle in the driveway. It was a relief because there were times in the past week that Keri and I thought we would never feel that relief again.

We went directly to our offices and, with new excitement, went immediately to work. Some of the greatest news was we had Ana back in the office. Dear sweet Ana, who spent last week cleaning houses every single day. It appeared that she was more relieved than we were to be back in the office.

Things were finally fixed and kind of back to normal. Keri, Mike, and I were relieved to not have to do Ana's job anymore.

Preparing the towels was nearly a full-time job for Ana. It was just something we found time to fit in during the course of the day last week, sometimes at 9:00 p.m. when we thought we were ready to leave the office. But truth be said, that job pretty much went to Mike. The result of his having to work almost full days preparing supplies resulted in the first time in ten years of our business I really saw happiness in Mike's eyes when he saw an employee. He looked at Ana with a new respect because he was able to go back to doing what he does well: coming in late, having a salad, and going home early.

It was a thrill to see so many people in the office that morning. We had to operate out of the norm and bring everyone in every day for that week because things were rearranged every day and there was no way we could pull their keys and files for three days. Not one day would be the usual schedule ever again. We did optimistically pull the keys and files for the teams for Monday and Tuesday.

We brought in all the new people at 7:00 a.m., and they were all there right on time. I couldn't believe it. We obtained two forms of identification that proved they were documented by the government to work for our company.

Ana helped them fill out their paperwork. She provided them with aprons and flew through explaining our supplies and how and where we use them. She told them how to use their aprons and told them what they need to do in each bathroom. It was verbal, certainly not written in their native language because we were not prepared for this. She then gave them the phone number to the office and further advised them if they had any questions while in the field to call the office. This was also the time before cell phones. If a cleaner needed to reach the office, they had to ask the customer if they could use the house phone. Looking back, I can only imagine the stress that must have caused, especially for employees who didn't speak English. Who were they supposed to ask? How were they supposed to explain what they needed when communication was already a struggle? At the time, I was so focused on getting the job done that I didn't spend nearly enough time trying to understand how my employees must have felt. I was thinking about operations. They were living the experience.

When the new teams arrived at the office who had worked together on Friday, we introduced them to their new third team member. Ana introduced the Spanish cleaner to their new team partners.

It was a bit chaotic, and there was a lot of complaining on both sides, which kind of surprised me because I thought the new Hispanic employees would just be thrilled to have a job and not complain, but they had the same concerns as the senior members had. How are they going to communicate, and no one is going to train them? Valid concerns that still resonate in my head today.

All I could think about was thank heaven Colleen was not there. She would've had every one of the cleaners, old and new, walking out of the office and refusing to clean that day under those circumstances. She would eventually calm down and realize that would mean she couldn't work either and come to her senses, but I was kind of glad I didn't have to go through that.

Eventually, we got everyone settled down, and they agreed to try and work as a team until I could get things fixed. I shared my solution with them, which was to spend the week looking for two bilingual supervisors and English-speaking or bilingual partners. I would then take the non-English speaking cleaners I just hired and put them with the new supervisors and the new English-speaking partners would be placed with the current teams.

That would utilize the extra cleaners we would actually have in the end. We needed an extra team to accomplish this, but we had three extra cars, so why not use them. Placing an extra person in each car left us with extra cars because we dismantled some teams. We were not adding another team. We were simply replacing a team. We were still short of an actual team number, but we had more people generating income.

The one thing that was so positive was the fact that this issue was created because Austin was growing so rapidly. The growth of new cleaning companies as well as the growth of clients looking for cleaning.

We had not called back a single client requesting a quote from the previous week, and we had a lot of new openings to fill the following week. Keri spent the entire day booking jobs for our new "imaginary" teams and rearranging schedules. She moved some clients, those who didn't mind which cleaner came as long as the job was done well, to the teams we didn't technically have yet. That we were always able to do.

Booking "in the blind" was never foreign to me. If you think back to what I said about our first two hundred customers, most of them were booked that way. We didn't know exactly who would clean the home yet, but we knew the job would get done. I had passed that faith on to Keri: Book the work and we would find a way to staff it. Overbooking was rarely the real problem, underbooking was. Every time you stretched a little and booked more than felt comfortable, two cancellations would show up and solve the problem for you. But if you underbooked, those same two cancellations could still happen, and now you had cleaners standing around with not enough hours. That's how you lose good people.

Nancy, one of the managers who later replaced Keri, used to say the most important thing she learned from me was, "Book 'em, we'll get 'em cleaned." In my consulting years, I saw this as a major issue in other companies. Owners were afraid to book ahead because they were afraid of being overbooked. That fear kept them small. Maybe the pressure of being stretched is what pushed me to hire and onboard cleaners faster and to figure out better systems to support them, I'm not sure. But I do know this: I once worked with a company that had twenty-four cleaners on payroll and only booked enough work for fourteen because "that's how many usually showed up." They had no attendance standards, no consequences, and no urgency to fix it. The result wasn't stability; it was chaos and lost opportunity.

My immediate concern, however, was that we no longer had the ability to properly train new cleaners because communication had broken down. In a moment of desperation, I ordered Jeff Campbell's training video that had been dubbed into Spanish. It was barely adequate in English, and in Spanish, it was even worse, but at the time, I didn't know that. How could I? I couldn't speak Spanish, much less understand it. What I did know was that I needed bilingual supervisors in place immediately.

By Thursday, I had hired two bilingual supervisors. I also found a couple of experienced Spanish-speaking cleaners who spoke enough English, maybe 50 percent or more, to work alongside English-speaking teams and maintain at least some level of communication. As we reorganized, something important clicked for me. A supervisor didn't need to be a driver. A driver needed a valid license and a clean driving record. A supervisor needed to supervise the team. In fact, it was often better if the supervisor didn't drive at all. They could use that riding time to review notes; handle paperwork; or, today, input information on a phone, prepare for the next job, and even help the driver with directions. It eliminated downtime and made the entire operation more efficient.

Through these changes, I was able to create a workable level of engagement among team members and a sense of patience and understanding from our clients as we transitioned into the new format. Ironically, that realization about separating the roles of driver and supervisor also spared me from what could have been a very expensive lawsuit, one I'll cover later.

CHAPTER 8

METICULOUSLY MANAGING THE DETAILS

A decade into my entrepreneurial journey, our company reached a significant milestone: We were generating an impressive annual revenue of $1 million. The once-tumultuous seas of entrepreneurship had finally calmed, and much of that stability stemmed from the remarkable office manager, Keri, who supported me in overseeing our increasingly complex operation. With a staff of twenty-four individuals, including ten dedicated working supervisors, we had become a well-oiled machine by 1996.

But as the business grew, our space needed to grow with us. Our little warehouse office had served its purpose well, but the endless mountains of towels (this was long before microfiber) were beginning to overwhelm the place. Back then, we used thick white terry towels, the kind that showed every speck of dirt. They got dingy fast, which meant constant washing and heavy bleaching just to keep them looking clean. We bought bleach by the case. For readers who have only ever used microfiber, it's hard to imagine, but those towels created an enormous laundry operation. At one point, we were processing nearly six thousand towels a week.

After two years, the landlord approached me and, with the gentle tact of a man trying to protect his plumbing, told me his septic system simply couldn't handle the volume of bleach we were using. As a farmer's daughter, I understood septic tanks better than most business owners, so while I was stunned, I also couldn't argue.

Ironically, microfiber towels became available shortly after we found the new office. We made the switch immediately, and everything changed. Another irony, microfiber towels couldn't be bleached; but they cleaned better, lasted longer, and required far fewer towels per home. Almost overnight, our weekly towel volume dropped from 6,000 to about 2,600. The ripple effects were huge. Regina, who had been working fifty-four hours a week managing mountains of laundry, often with overtime, dropped to a thirty-six-hour week. For the first time, she had the margin in her schedule to do more than just keep up. She began manually calculating efficiency rates for every team, every week—numbers we later used in one-on-one meetings to coach performance and improve consistency. What started as a plumbing problem ended up becoming an operational upgrade that made us more efficient, more scalable, and more repeatable.

I looked into the cost of outsourcing the laundry. But Pat, our supplies supervisor at that time, was already doing the work efficiently; and outsourcing would cost almost what we were already spending. Besides, we relied on those extra four hours a day to keep Pat busy. She washed towels, filled supply bottles, prepped equipment, restocked materials and was our main relief cleaner. Losing that would create more problems than it solved.

So, once again, we went office hunting. Thanks to my chamber connections, I went to see Henry Mayes, a real estate agent I trusted. I told him we needed something inexpensive, practical, and zoned commercial.

He looked at me thoughtfully and said, "Why are you renting? Why don't you buy?"

I laughed. "Because I don't have the down payment."

He grinned. "You don't need one. Just assume someone's mortgage for five years. Then the property is yours."

"What? That's possible?"

"Absolutely. Let me find you something."

Incredible. Who knew?

Henry found a small house zoned as Commercial S, listed at $50,000. I nearly fell over. It had an attached garage, perfect for supplies, and although it was tiny (1,100 square feet, the same size as our house), it had everything we needed: bedrooms that could become offices, a dedicated laundry room, water lines, legal zoning, and…thick pink shag carpeting that should've been declared a national disaster. It was dirty, outdated, and, frankly, should have been bulldozed. But it was ours. And after looking at beautiful $180,000 offices that needed work anyway, buying this one was the smartest decision we could make.

We assumed the owners' mortgage, apparently they were about to lose the place, and moved out of our warehouse headquarters.

Buying the building turned out to be one of the best decisions for our business. We customized it exactly as we needed. The entire garage became a dedicated supplies room with a counter. Only the supplies person was allowed behind it. Everything was handed over the counter, controlled, precise, and accountable. No more missing bottles or wandering products.

As the company grew, we expanded the office. Eventually, we built a separate structure behind the original building. That addition gave me a real executive office and one for Mike as well. The center became a beautiful meeting and training room furnished with the high-end pieces that once lived in my home. (I always believe in recycling good furniture.)

Recruiting instantly improved. Cleaners walked in and saw professionalism, polish, and scale. We became the most impressive cleaning service in town, not because we were the biggest (which we were) but because we looked like we belonged with the biggest. For seven years, we didn't place a single job ad. People simply walked in, told friends, or sent relatives.

And there was another silver lining. Many years later, during a difficult period when Mike and I were arguing too much, I considered selling the business. The valuation came back at $1.4 million, and the reason we could command that much had less to do with mops, buckets, and clients and more to do with real estate. The property had skyrocketed in value to $400,000, and a Lexus dealer behind us wanted the land. When we eventually divorced, Mike kept both the business and the property. He was indeed offered $400,000 for the building, and upon purchase, they promptly tore it down.

Selling a home-service business is hard. There's no real equity. Clients can disappear overnight, much like companies with no real assets losing value in the stock market. But a building? That always appreciates. My advice: If you run a home-service business, buy your office. It's one of the best write-offs you'll ever have and one of the smartest long-term assets you can own.

Amid all this progress and consistency though, we were suddenly faced with a significant challenge: replacing our long-time supplies person, Pat. She had decided to retire and move with her husband to Florida. She was unforgettable, slow, accident-prone, and capable of breaking almost anything; but she showed up every day, never late, never absent. She shook the lint out of six thousand towels weekly and then folded them with a level of consistency we depended on. She could cause chaos almost anywhere, like the day she shattered a toilet seat while retrieving a five-pound can of coffee from a shelf above it. The sound of something breaking was our unofficial signal that Pat was in the room. Despite her quirks, replacing her was nearly impossible.

Then, one day, Regina walked into the office. With maybe ten English words in her vocabulary, she was an unlikely candidate. But within two days, she proved herself invaluable. She worked fast, meticulously, quietly, and with incredible pride. She took notes, written in Spanish and completely unreadable to us, but her results didn't need translating.

Regina handled washing, drying, and folding those six thousand towels in two days instead of a week. We gradually added office cleaning, bottle refills, trash removal, and supply prep. What took Pat forty hours took Regina twenty. To keep her at a full forty hours, we expanded her responsibilities even more.

One of our biggest operational frustrations had been towel tracking. Under Pat, recordkeeping was casual at best. We routinely lost 150 towels a month. We couldn't charge teams without creating tension, and clients were constantly calling because we forgot a towel in their home. One client, on her third phone call about a fifty-cent towel we had left at her home that she subsequently left on her patio, eventually pushed me over the edge.

"Ma'am, I understand you're concerned about the towel," I said, trying to keep my voice even.

"Well, it's been sitting on my patio for three days now!" she snapped.

"I apologize for that. We can send someone to pick it up or—"

"I've called three times about this!"

I took a deep breath. "If it's bothering you that much, please throw it away."

Silence on the other end. Then, "Well, I never…"

"I'm sorry, but we can't keep sending people out for a fifty-cent towel. If you'd like to cancel your service, I understand."

That ended the relationship, but it also marked the day I vowed to fix our system.

With Regina, everything changed. She counted towels out and counted towels back. She noted condition. If "dirty" towels were dry, she flagged it, meaning a team probably cut corners. We could address issues before the client found them. It was a consistent proactive quality control tool that happened every time a team checked in.

Our operation ran in teams of three. On Tuesdays and Thursdays, check-in/check-out days, all sixteen teams returned to the office. These were exhausting days. Teams reported their supply needs by noon. Regina prepared everything: towels, floor Shwipes, keys, files, maps, response cards. This was before smartphones or software. Everything was physical: paper files, client notes, MapQuest printouts, or hand-drawn maps. Keys were checked out and checked back in, almost three hundred per week. We developed a two-step system: Regina pulled the keys and files; supervisors double-checked her. Mistakes were costly when dealing with a city the size of Austin, but the system caught virtually everything.

Towel counting transformed everything. Complaints dropped. Inventory stabilized. The first time we charged cleaners for missing towels, they were furious. They asked if they could bring them in the next week.

"Of course," I said. "Bring them in and I'll refund the money."

The very next week, they returned 175 extra towels, and suddenly, missing towels became rare.

What initially looked like a dull, tedious task, counting towels turned out to be one of the most important operational systems we ever put in place. Tracking towels reduced expenses, improved quality, prevented complaints, and even helped us identify which teams needed coaching. When towels went missing repeatedly, it was rarely an accident. It pointed to a breakdown somewhere in the process, and that information mattered.

I know several large companies today, about the size we were then, that attempted towel tracking and eventually abandoned it. They told me it was too labor intensive, too frustrating, too hard to maintain. But year after year, I watched our production grow while our complaint numbers stayed steady. Theirs didn't. Systems only work when they are maintained consistently, especially the small ones that seem insignificant on the surface.

Lost towels don't just affect inventory, they affect clients. A towel left behind becomes a phone call. A phone call becomes irritating. Enough small irritations become a complaint. And enough complaints, no matter how minor they seem, erode trust. Trust isn't lost in one dramatic moment; it's worn down by repeated lapses in attention.

Success in the cleaning business doesn't come from dramatic moves or clever ideas. It comes from managing the tiny, unglamorous details that everyone else ignores and building systems that make those details repeatable. When the little things are handled the same way every time, quality becomes predictable. And predictable quality is what keeps clients coming back.

That kind of consistency is what holds a company together as it grows. It keeps systems reliable, people accountable, and the client experience steady, even when volume increases.

CHAPTER 9

THE COST OF NOT TRAINING WELL

Once systems are in place, they begin to expose something far more uncomfortable than missing towels or blown engines. They expose assumptions. They reveal where clarity ends and guesswork begins. And they make it painfully obvious that consistency does not come from intention; it comes from understanding.

I had spent years building systems that worked because I stayed close to them. But as soon as I tried to step back, delegating tasks I didn't enjoy or no longer had time to manage, the cracks appeared. Not because people didn't care. Not because they weren't capable. But because I had confused showing with training and trust with verification.

Regina was the person who made that distinction impossible for me to ignore.

Working with her forced me to slow down, rethink my shortcuts, and confront how often I assumed comprehension simply because a task seemed obvious to me. When language barriers entered the picture, every weak spot in my training process surfaced immediately. There was no room for vague explanations, rushed demonstrations, or "You'll figure it out as you go."

Regina didn't just perform tasks, she reflected my training back to me. Whatever wasn't clear became evident in the results. Whatever wasn't reinforced showed up as inconsistency. And whatever I failed to inspect quietly became my responsibility anyway.

It was during this period that I learned one of the most expensive lessons of my career: The cost of not training well is never limited to the task you're trying to delegate. It shows up later, louder, and usually at the worst possible moment.

I vividly recall the day I thought she was ready to take on the task of checking the oil in our company cars, a responsibility I had been eager to delegate. Checking the oil was a job I disliked. It always seemed like Mike was absent during the crucial oil-checking window on Tuesday and Thursday afternoons; and Keri, our office manager, was already buried in supervisor questions, missing keys, missing files, missing checks, anything that could go wrong after a couple of days of cleaning.

Meanwhile, I was trying to conduct one-on-one sessions with each team, which I treated as sacred and uninterrupted time. Yet somehow, oil checks kept landing in my lap.

Early in my business journey, I had learned a crucial lesson from a commanding boss: "Inspect what you suspect and suspect everything."

At first, I placed immense trust in everyone across nearly every aspect of the business. I even entrusted cleaners with our brand-new GEO Metros. Remember how that worked out for me with the upholstery holes? Well, there's more.

One fateful day, a team called in to report their car was smoking and wouldn't start. When Mike investigated, it turned out they were correct: The engine had blown up due to lack of oil.

Firing them wasn't a practical solution. They were excellent cleaners, but they were not proactive in car maintenance. That day marked the beginning of my routine: Personally checking the oil in every company car every week.

I kept two spare vehicles to replace any that needed oil changes, which we managed in-house. I only had to lose one engine before realizing the importance of that procedure and the wisdom behind, "Inspect what you suspect and suspect everything."

Now here's where Regina comes in.

One day I decided to teach Regina how to check the oil and add more if needed. The lesson felt simple. When she finished, I put the hood down, walked away, and went back to my one-on-ones, thinking, *Honestly, how hard could it be to check the oil in a car?*

Sometime later, my intercom buzzed. Keri's voice came through, urgent.

"Sharon, I'm sorry to interrupt, but you need to take this call."

"Can it wait?" I asked. "I'm in the middle of a one-on-one."

"No. It can't. One of the supervisors is calling, and she sounds distressed."

I picked up the phone. "This is Sharon."

"Sharon!" the supervisor's voice was panicked. "We're in the Outback Steakhouse parking lot, and our car's hood just flew off!"

"What? The hood flew off? Are you okay?"

"We're fine, but the hood is just…gone. It flew off while we were driving."

It was so strange it didn't even feel real. I called Mike and told him to meet the team at the parking lot. I planned to deal with it after I finished my one-on-one, which was already going poorly and required my full attention.

Then Keri buzzed again.

"Sharon, I'm so sorry, but you really need to take this one too."

I sighed. "Now what?"

"It's another team. Their hood came off too. They're on the side of Highway 183."

That was more dramatic than the Outback parking lot. I told Keri to page Mike and reroute him to Highway 183.

By this point, the puzzle pieces were starting to come together, but before I could investigate further, my office door burst open, an unprecedented occurrence when my door was closed.

In walked a cleaning team, holding a car hood in their hands.

When I saw that hood, I burst into uncontrollable laughter. Tears streamed down my face. All I could do was laugh. If only we had seven-second reels back then, because this was certainly one.

This was nobody's fault but mine.

The hoods on the GEO Metros were peculiar. They required a double closure. For some inexplicable reason, the first closure only hooked the hood, while the second press secured it entirely. Perhaps it was a safety feature, but it was certainly not foolproof.

Regina had closed all the hoods to the first closure, as she had been taught, but not the secure second closure.

We lost three hoods that day before we identified the problem and the solution.

It was an expensive lesson, but it taught me something bigger than car maintenance. It taught me that when you train entry-level employees, "almost right" is not right. "They'll figure it out" is not training. And anything you do not teach clearly becomes your responsibility later, usually at the worst possible moment.

Not long after that, another training challenge hit me, one that couldn't be solved with a hood latch: client complaints.

In my previous role at MCI, complaints rarely reached my desk. There were layers between me and the customer: representatives, supervisors, customer service departments. But in this business, at least in the beginning, there was no buffer.

Until Keri joined the office, I was the sole recipient of every complaint, every frustration, every unmet expectation.

I didn't necessarily blame the cleaners, but I did blame myself. I wasn't paying attention to the little things, or for that matter, the big things, when it came to cleaner training.

And I didn't particularly want to learn it.

But I had even less desire to personally clean houses, so I decided I had better embrace a truth that annoyed me: If I wasn't going to do the cleaning, I had to learn how to teach it.

If I was going to survive, I needed to figure out how to train cleaners to consistently meet our clients' expectations, especially those of our typical repeat client.

That realization collided head-on with how we were operating in the beginning.

When we first opened The Upstairs Maid, we truly tried to be everything to everyone. My business cards actually said personalized cleaning service, and we meant it. If a client wanted ironing, we did ironing. If they wanted laundry done, we did laundry. Whatever they asked for, we said yes.

At that point, we had five part-time cleaners who had been with the company for a long time. They had inherited the thirty clients we purchased along with the business; and over time, they had built strong, comfortable relationships with them. They were attentive in their own way. They arranged clothes neatly, pointed all the shoes in the closet in the same direction, and lined up shoes on the floor so everything matched.

Those clients were satisfied, but not for the reason I initially thought.

What I came to understand was that these relationships had matured together. The cleaners and the clients had grown used to one another's habits, preferences, and idiosyncrasies. Some clients didn't care much about how the home was cleaned; what mattered to them was the familiarity. In many cases, they were older, sometimes lonely, and genuinely enjoyed the company. They didn't mind pointing out what had been missed. Some even liked it. It gave them a sense of involvement, a feeling of control, and for a certain type of client, that dynamic worked just fine.

But it wasn't scalable.

When we first opened our doors, during those first four weeks, I didn't receive a single complaint. I remember thinking, these cleaners really know what they're doing. But the truth was simpler than that. I haven't been selling yet. I was inheriting relationships.

The complaints started when I went out and brought in new clients.

That's when the pattern became clear. You can build rapport based on personality with about 20 percent of your client base. That was about how many clients stuck with the previous owners. Those clients don't really care how the house gets cleaned; they just want to know their cleaners. The relationship is the service.

The other 80 percent want something different: They want a clean house.

They may appreciate a friendly rapport, but it is secondary. What they are paying for is results. Consistency. The same friendly team needs to clean the house the same perfect way every time.

That was the moment I realized we hadn't built a cleaning company yet. We had built a collection of personal relationships.

And while relationships matter, they cannot be the foundation of a business that needs to grow.

There was a lot of organizing and detailing to our cleanings. What there wasn't a lot of was cleaning.

I learned that quickly, especially as complaints began rolling in. We were learning in the dark and sometimes learning fast hurts.

One client said, "I don't care if they match all my shoes in the closet and point them in the same direction. What I want them to do is get the damn ring out of the toilet."

That sentence stopped me cold.

And she was right.

What she wanted was not organization. What she wanted was a clean house. Organization companies already existed. That wasn't who we were supposed to be. Cleaning was the job. Cleaning was the promise.

That phone call made something very clear to me. Good intentions don't equal good results. Effort without direction doesn't serve the client. And allowing everyone to do things their own way doesn't create quality; it creates inconsistency.

But that wasn't the only wake-up call.

Another came a few weeks later, and it was one I will never forget.

It was the end of the day, long after normal business hours. The phone rang, and as I often did back then, I answered.

"Hello, this is The Upstairs Maid."

A woman's voice came through, calm as could be. "This is Valerie McKinney, and I think your girls vacuumed up my husband today."

For a moment, I was certain I had misheard her.

"I'm sorry, excuse me?"

She repeated it, the same way.

And this time, I understood every word.

My heart sank. I immediately apologized and asked her what made her think that had happened.

She explained that her husband's ashes had been sitting on the fireplace mantel. She had recently spread some of the ashes and, in her grief, hadn't sealed the container afterward. She believed the container must have fallen to the floor. When the cleaners vacuumed, they unknowingly vacuumed up what she described as black ashes, ashes that were very clearly human remains to someone familiar with cremated remains.

Evidently, that was not our cleaning staff.

It was surreal, bizarre—and horrifying.

I told her I was so sorry and that we would figure it out immediately. I hung up and called the cleaning team that had been in her home that day. I asked them if they had changed the vacuum bag.

They hadn't.

I drove to the cleaner's home, retrieved her vacuum, and carefully removed the bag. I brought it back to our house and laid newspapers across our dining room table. I placed the bag on top of the paper and slowly opened it.

Mike and I sifted through the contents gently removing clusters of normal household debris, pet hair, lint, dirt.

What we were left with was fine black dust that appeared to be remains, part of a body.

We separated what we could, placed it carefully into a small bag, and brought it back to Mrs. McKinney.

She thanked me profusely.

She did not cancel her service.

That moment stayed with me for years. In fact, it still does. Most clients, I learned again and again, are far more forgiving than we give them credit for, especially when we show up, take responsibility, and handle even the most unimaginable situations with care and respect.

But here's what I didn't fully realize at the time: The solution to preventing situations like that was already forming in my mind, even if I couldn't see it clearly yet.

Our cleaners were carrying everything in their hands, spray bottles, towels, scrapers, tile brushes, five things in one hand and five in the other. They had no free hands. If something started to fall, a picture frame, a canister, a decorative item on a mantel, they had no way to catch it. Their hands were already full of stuff. They could only watch it hit the floor.

If they'd had aprons with pockets, like the ones I would eventually introduce after doing my research and finding a better system, they would have had a free hand. That canister might not have fallen. Or if it started to tip, the cleaner could have caught it with their free hand.

The aprons weren't just about organization or efficiency; they were about preventing accidents, real ones, like vacuuming up someone's husband.

I didn't see that connection then. But looking back now, I realize that moment was one more piece of evidence pointing toward the same conclusion: We didn't just need cleaners. We needed focused training. Real training. Training that taught people what mattered most and gave them the tools to do it right.

And once again, I didn't blame the cleaners.

I blamed myself, for not being more engaged, for not addressing complaints sooner, for not putting a real training structure in place.

I still had no desire to clean houses myself, but I now understood that if I didn't learn how to teach cleaning correctly, the business would never stabilize.

That was when I went looking for information on how to clean properly and how to train cleaners to clean properly.

CHAPTER 10

TRAINING BEFORE THE FIRST HOUSE

When I decided to learn how to teach cleaning correctly, I had one problem: There wasn't a lot of help available.

There were no YouTube channels to binge. No online academies. No industry groups handing out cleaning procedures. There was mostly trial and error, other owners who guarded their systems like state secrets, and a whole lot of people winging it and calling it training.

So I went to the local library.

In 1988, I found three books on house cleaning. I checked them out and later purchased them. They were written by Jeff Campbell, and although they omitted details like ceiling fans, cobwebs, and baseboards, they offered something I desperately needed: a structured framework.

For that, I will always be grateful to Jeff Campbell. He gave me a foundation I could build on, a process strong enough to support a real business, not just a hustle.

I studied his method and appreciated the logic behind it. But I also realized something quickly: A process only works if you give people the tools to carry it out.

One tool in particular mattered more than I expected: the apron.

Jeff Campbell sold an apron alongside his process. I bought one. But I couldn't afford twenty-four more, and I already knew Mike wouldn't approve that expense.

Once again, my mother came to the rescue.

I sent her the fabric, and she painstakingly made twenty-three aprons identical to the one I had purchased. They were intricate, with pockets designed for specific tools; long, narrow pockets for a tile brush; a smaller one for a razor-blade scraper; and several larger pockets and loops.

In about two weeks, she shipped them to me.

Armed with those aprons and that process, I rolled out what, at the time, felt like an enormous training experiment.

I took each cleaner individually to my home and had them watch Jeff Campbell's video for the area they would be cleaning. Then I showed them what the video didn't include: long dusting, ceiling fans, other details that mattered in a real home.

They cleaned each area while I observed closely. I didn't just watch their hands. I watched their sequence. I watched where they hesitated. I watched what they skipped without noticing.

During this period, I had twenty-four cleaners.

For a month, I placed mustard, ketchup, dust, and dirt in various areas of my home and let it dry overnight. The next day, the cleaner had to tackle those spots. They resisted the new system at first. Most people resist change when they've never been taught why it matters.

But by the time they left my house, they usually warmed up to it, because they could feel the difference. They were faster. They missed less. They had fewer "Oh, I forgot that" moments.

And the apron, oddly enough, became a key part of both quality and efficiency. Almost a deal-breaker too.

When it came time to introduce the aprons, Colleen announced she wouldn't wear one. She said it during a meeting, and her stance quickly gained followers.

At the time, of the twenty-four cleaners, Colleen carried the most influence.

"Next you'll have us wearing dresses like Molly Maids," she said, arms crossed. She threatened to quit rather than wear an apron.

Molly Maids required aprons, and at the time, they also required dresses: gray dresses, white collars, short sleeves, white cuffs, and a lace apron to finish the uniform.

I believe Molly Maids was trying to create a branding connection to Hazel, the famous live-in maid from the 1960s sitcom. But the uniform created a different problem. Men would show up behind cleaners when they bent over to clean, which made the decision-maker in the home, usually the wife, very uncomfortable.

Eventually, Molly Maids allowed slacks under the dresses. This was not a time when leggings were common, and tights were basically nylons. So the cleaners ended up wearing bulky black pants under dresses. It was uncomfortable and impractical.

That dress code did not last.

Our aprons needed to.

Despite the resistance, everyone eventually embraced the idea, even if they didn't love the aprons themselves. Colleen was willing to try a different apron because she believed in the concept. She had two young children at home and wanted to get home to them. She knew this system would make her faster without sacrificing quality.

As a leader in our organization, Colleen needed to support the apron system. So I listened to her preferences. She was slender, and the narrow pockets poked her ribs when she bent. Susan and about 85 percent of our other cleaners were also slim from the pace of the work.

Colleen wanted three large pockets instead so she could store her tools in one place and access them easily.

I agreed.

I contacted my "sweat shop" in Wisconsin, my mother, and asked her to adjust them. It wasn't easy to deliver that message, but she handled it with grace. She stayed up late sewing and had new aprons ready within a week.

The cleaners loved them.

Years later, I got a moment that proved how completely the culture had changed.

One morning, I was preparing for a chamber meeting when the front door swung open. I heard footsteps heading toward my office, and Colleen appeared in the doorway.

"I left my apron at home," she said, "and I'm not gonna buy another one. I'm also not gonna work today without an apron, so you might as well just give me one."

We looked at each other and burst into laughter.

The woman who once threatened to quit rather than wear an apron now refused to clean without one.

That moment stayed with me, not because of the apron but because it exposed something bigger. When training is missing or incomplete, even the simplest improvement feels like a threat. When training is done right, change becomes inevitable.

At the time, I didn't fully grasp how rare that kind of training was in our industry. I assumed others were doing what we were doing, teaching process, procedure, and the "why" behind the work.

I assumed wrong.

And that's when I began refining what training needed to be, if it was going to work.

Here's what I learned, long before I had fancy materials or any kind of polished "program": About 70 percent of training needs to happen in the office, and only about 30 percent belongs in the field.

That might surprise people, because most companies do the opposite. They throw trainees into houses and call it training.

But the field isn't where learning begins.

You can't repeat it calmly when a client is home. You can't repeat it when you're racing a clock. You can't repeat it when a trainer is whispering instructions while trying not to interrupt the flow of a paid clean.

But repetition is exactly how people learn.

Office training, done correctly, builds familiarity before the cleaner ever walks into a house. It reduces confusion, reduces trainer frustration, and prevents the panic spiral that happens when the trainee is overwhelmed and the trainer feels like they're dragging a dead weight through a day's schedule.

And I learned something else that changed everything.

Training works best when it is focused.

One area at a time.

Back then, I had three-person teams. That meant I could train someone on the bathroom, and if they were capable, I could train that bathroom person in a day and get them out on a team. In a three-person team, that's all they needed to learn at first.

Once they learned about that area, most of them liked it so much they didn't want to move. And, honestly, that was a good thing.

When people consistently cleaned the same area, we had less breakage and less damage. They learned where things belonged. They learned the "personality" of that room. They got fast. They got confident.

It wasn't glamorous; it was practical.

And it worked.

That's also why I became very clear about where training should happen.

You teach process first in a repeat home, not a deep clean.

A deep clean hides the process because you can be inside one tub forever. The sequence disappears. Everything feels urgent, and the cleaner's brain is drowning in "what next."

But in a repeat home, the kind of home they normally clean, process becomes visible. Predictable. Measurable.

And if you are retraining, be sure it is in a repeat home they personally clean. There's nowhere to hide. If there's buildup on a windowsill, they can't blame the previous cleaner, because they were the previous cleaner. When they see their own missed dirt, most good cleaners care.

That moment humbles them in a productive way.

And this is where you have to be clear: It isn't their fault. They missed it because they didn't have a sequence. They didn't know what they didn't know.

Now they do.

And once they have a process, they shouldn't miss it again, not because they're perfect but because the steps guide them to the same places every time.

That's the difference between hope and consistency.

Process is the order.

Procedure is the "how."

Process is what you clean first, second, third. Procedure is the tools, products, and actions used to clean what you just arrived at.

Most companies teach procedure first because it feels urgent: "Which bottle do I use? Which towel? What do I do with this?" Procedure overwhelms process in the field every time.

So the steps have to be simple enough to carry on a small piece of paper in their apron pocket.

I found that trainees learned better when they wrote the steps themselves and kept them on a small piece of paper in their apron pocket. Those are process steps, not procedures. That one act of writing them down improved comprehension, recall, and long-term consistency.

Then you teach procedures through a manual presented in process order so the manual reinforces the sequence they just learned. Pictures matter. Familiarity comes from repetition. You don't list every product in the company. You list what's used in that room, in that step, in that moment.

And then you test.

A quiz isn't punishment; it's proof. Proof they understood. Proof they're ready to step into the field without the trainer hovering like a chef watching someone bake a cake for the first time.

Because that's the goal. The trainer shouldn't be telling them every single solitary thing to do. The trainer should be able to watch and then ask one question.

The role of the trainer changes dramatically when you move from double-shadow training to what I came to call single-shadow training.

In double shadowing, the trainer cleans while the trainee watches. When the roles reverse, the trainer shadows the trainee, and because the trainee has only seen the process once, the trainer feels compelled to narrate every move.

"Pick up your towel."

"Start with the sink."

"Don't forget the fixtures."

The instructions come before the trainee even has a chance to think.

That style of training feels helpful. It feels efficient. But it is completely counterproductive.

When 75 percent of the process and procedure is taught in the office, the trainer's role in the field fundamentally changes: Say nothing, observe. That was a paradigm shift for an industry conditioned to believe training requires constant instruction.

If the trainee does everything correctly, you say exactly one thing: "Great job." And you mean it. Some people don't need correction. They learned from the videos. They studied the manual. They absorbed the sequence. All they need is confirmation that what they did was right.

That doesn't make the trainer ineffective. It makes the trainee exceptional.

The real discipline of training shows up when something is missed.

Imagine a trainee working through step 6 in the bathroom, the wipe-and-shine stage, where details matter. The toilet paper holder is part of that step. If the trainee walks past it and moves on to the next area, every instinct in you will want to speak.

Don't.

You already know what they missed. That's not the question.

The question is whether they know.

If you immediately point it out, two things happen, and neither of them helps. First, you teach them to rely on you instead of their own awareness. Second, you rob them of the opportunity to build the habit that actually matters: noticing.

You are not going to follow this person forever. You will not be there every time they miss something. The only way they stop missing it is if they catch it.

And here's what happens when you wait.

They move into the next bathroom, and when they see the same item, they pause. You see it in their face, the smile, the slight nod, the moment of recognition. They go back and get it.

Now you have something powerful to say: "Nice catch. You remembered."

That compliment sticks. They will never forget it again.

But if you rush in every time and say, "You forgot the toilet paper holder," they will continue to forget it. You'll get frustrated. They'll get discouraged. And the habit will cement itself, not because they're careless but because you never let them own the correction.

There's another reason to wait: Sometimes they were about to go back for it. If you jump in too fast and say, "What did you miss?" before they've clearly moved on, you're likely to get a defensive response: "I was going to get that."

And maybe they were. Do not take away their opportunity to sign. That might make them defensive.

That pause, that uncomfortable silence, is the hardest part of being a trainer: Knowing when not to guide. Knowing when to let the process work.

Because that's the goal.

The trainer should not be telling someone every single thing to do. The trainer should be able to observe, and then ask one simple question: "What did you miss?"

It sounds easy.

It isn't.

The difficulty isn't asking the question; the difficulty is waiting long enough to allow the new trainee to gain some praise and then praise them because when you do, you just gave them something most entry-level cleaners don't get enough of: pride.

Don't steal that moment. Let them earn it.

At that point, training is no longer something you do to them. It becomes something they do for themselves.

Retraining, however, is a different animal entirely.

Everything I've described so far is easier when you're working with unseasoned trainees, people who have never cleaned professionally or who are new to your company. New hires expect change. Their habits aren't fully formed yet, so resistance is lower.

Experienced cleaners are another story.

Retraining asks people to unlearn behaviors they've relied on for years. That is never comfortable. If someone has never worn an apron, their hands will instinctively put tools down on cabinets, chairs, or countertops, exactly where they've always put them. If they're used to rinsing and immediately shining, they will want to do that again, because that's what feels right. The idea that they can walk away and come back later, without sacrificing time or quality, takes time to accept.

Retraining is not about intelligence or effort; it's about habits.

And habits don't change just because someone is told to do something different. Some research suggests difficult habits can take over two hundred repetitions to become natural. Easier ones may shift in as few as seventeen. In my experience, adopting a new cleaning system takes about two weeks for an experienced cleaner, if the process is taught correctly.

Habits change when the thinking behind the habit changes. Change their thinking and you will change their beliefs and actions.

That's why retraining requires a shift in how the trainer approaches the process. You cannot simply demonstrate new actions and expect them to stick. Your job when retraining is to spend more time explaining why the actions are different than explaining the actions themselves.

Success in retraining also depends on where it happens.

Retrain in a repeat home, a home a cleaner has just cleaned recently and always cleans. Make sure you are training in the area they normally clean. Especially with stubborn cleaners who believe they already know everything there is to know.

What we don't want to hear when we encounter a particularly dirty area is, "This isn't my home. My homes don't look like this." Their own repeat home removes every excuse. If there is dust on a windowsill or buildup on a fixture, they can't blame a previous cleaner, because they were the previous cleaner. Familiarity makes missed areas obvious when a consistent process is applied.

When experienced cleaners see their own missed work laid out plainly in front of them, something shifts. Most good cleaners care deeply about doing a good job. That realization doesn't demoralize them, it motivates them.

Suddenly, retraining is no longer about being corrected; it becomes about improvement.

When a cleaner understands the reason behind the change and sees the impact in a home they know well, engagement rises. Training in one kitchen, one bathroom, and one living area is usually enough. If it takes longer, you likely have a buy-in problem, not a training problem. At that point, more one-on-one conversation matters more than more instruction.

Understanding alone isn't enough. They must believe in the system.

Without buy-in, a cleaner may perform correctly while you're watching, but won't repeat the process when you're gone. Compliance without belief never lasts.

The moment you're looking for doesn't happen during training. It happens afterward.

It's when an experienced cleaner goes into the next home alone, follows the process without prompting, and comes back saying, "I shaved fifteen minutes off that kitchen, and it was cleaner."

That's buy-in.

At that point, retraining is complete, not because habits are perfect, but because the cleaner has experienced the benefit personally: speed, quality, ease, confidence.

That's how you end up with people like Colleen, cleaners who once resisted the apron and later refused to work without one. Not because it was required, but because it worked.

Retraining done right doesn't create obedience. It creates ownership.

And ownership is what lasts. That's when complaints begin to fade, not because people suddenly became different but because they finally had what they were missing: a repeatable road map.

CHAPTER 11

THE UNFORESEEN TRUTH

Throughout my extensive career, which spanned the management of thousands of individuals, one enduring reality became abundantly clear: Human honesty remains an enigmatic and unpredictable trait. Despite my confidence in deciphering people's motives and character, the fundamental attribute of integrity often eluded my grasp. I encountered surprise after surprise, prompting me to appreciate the value of concrete evidence when it came to discerning guilt or innocence, particularly in cases involving theft. The pivotal lesson on this subject crystallized during my tenure at MCI's expansive telemarketing center, a bustling hub furnished with cubicles, each equipped with workstations, personal computers, and telephones for our 350 dedicated sales representatives. As our operation burgeoned from an initially planned five hundred representatives to the colossal one thousand, I was tasked with overseeing them. My manager resisted the idea of recruiting additional management personnel. Instead, he continued to expand my responsibilities.

Recognizing the need for additional support, he eventually granted me the authority to promote three exceptional sales representatives to assistant positions. These remarkable individuals, who devoted four hours each day exclusively to assist me, possessed exceptional skills, often outperforming me in various tasks. Their intelligence, ambition, and competitiveness were undeniable. I had wholeheartedly capitalized on their capabilities, thus forging a profound understanding of their personalities. Life was good. I started working reasonable ten-hour days and consistently achieved my monthly performance bonuses. Then one day my path encountered a stumbling block when I inadvertently disclosed an employee's expected salary increase before its formal approval by the human resources department. This error led to an unexpected phone call from the regional director, David Palmer, inquiring about the situation.

"Sharon, what the hell happened?" David's voice boomed through the phone.

I took a deep breath. "I made a mistake. I told an employee about their raise before HR officially approved it."

"Jesus Christ. I knew I wasn't getting a cherry, but I sure didn't think I was getting a plum," he said, then abruptly hung up.

Fearing for my job, I immediately confided in my manager, who reassured me that David's response was characteristic of his personality and that my employment was secure.

Shortly thereafter, David contacted me again and instructed me to attend every management seminar available throughout the year. At the time, it felt like punishment. I had embarrassed the company, and this was my consequence. But looking back, it was one of the greatest gifts of my corporate career.

Those seminars sent me traveling to cities all over the country, many of them places where my college friends from UW-Oshkosh had landed after graduation. So, while I was officially there to learn about leadership, communication, and personnel management, I also managed to reconnect with old friends over dinners, laughter, and late-night conversations. What started as discipline quietly turned into one of the most enjoyable and formative years of my professional life.

Up to that point, most of what I knew about management had come from instinct and observation. These seminars gave structure to what I had only been guessing at. I learned how to give day-to-day feedback without humiliating someone, how to correct behavior without attacking the person, how to role-play difficult conversations before having them, how to explain policies so they felt fair instead of arbitrary. MCI didn't just tell us to manage people; they trained us how to communicate, how to set expectations, and how to hold people accountable while preserving dignity. That training became the backbone of everything I would later do as a business owner.

Those classes taught me that leadership isn't about authority; it's about clarity and consistency. People perform better when they understand what's expected, why it matters, and what happens if the standard isn't met. Policies aren't there to control people; they exist to protect fairness and make decisions predictable instead of emotional. Without realizing it, I was being handed the tools I would one day rely on to build training systems, conduct one-on-ones, and lead cleaners from every background imaginable.

At the time, I thought I was just trying to survive a reprimand. In reality, I was being prepared to run my own company. As my career at MCI continued an upward trajectory, an unexpected incident disrupted the harmonious flow. One of my supervisors approached me, concerned that one of her sales representatives reported missing money from her purse. Although I initially dismissed the incident as a simple case of misplaced funds, I conducted a cursory investigation by asking colleagues who shared workspace with the individual in question. Regrettably, the inquiries yielded no suspicious leads, and even my trusted assistants professed ignorance of any wrongdoing. Given the relatively modest sum involved, approximately $50 at the time (equivalent to around $150 today), I chose not to escalate the matter further. The situation appeared to resolve itself, and daily operations resumed without incident. However, this tranquility was short-lived, as another supervisor soon approached me with a similar complaint, yet another sales representative reported missing money. Faced with the recurrence of such incidents, my concern deepened, prompting me to escalate the matter to my superiors. My manager, recognizing the gravity of the situation, immediately took a proactive step by involving the local police. It was a decision that had never crossed my mind, but in retrospect, it proved to be the right one. MCI's reputation prompted the swift response of the police department, who dispatched detectives to our premises. Their meticulous examination included dusting for fingerprints, a procedure that would prove crucial. The meticulousness of the police investigation was astonishing, and I couldn't be more grateful for their diligence. It was during this initial experience managing theft that I learned the paramount importance of relying solely on facts, unburdened by emotions or conjecture. To my astonishment, the evidence pointed unequivocally to one of my three dedicated assistants, a junior at UT, a stellar student, hailing from a prosperous Dallas family, adorned in opulent attire, and the embodiment of beauty. Yet she was a thief, revealing the insidious nature of such compulsions, which therapy and potential incarceration alone could hope to mitigate. Her identification as the perpetrator defied my expectations, serving as a poignant lesson that left an indelible mark on my career.

I am so grateful for the lesson I learned at MCI because it certainly gave me the accurate direction I needed. In the early stages of any home service company, there comes a dreaded day when an unsettling incident forces its way into the picture. For me, this momentous day arrived relatively soon after launching our cleaning business, approximately nine months after we first opened our doors. It was marked by an unsettling phone call from one of our clients, a prominent attorney whose husband was an even more prominent attorney, who reported the disappearance of a valuable $10,000 tennis bracelet from their residence.

"Ms. Butza, this is Mrs. Henderson." The voice on the phone was cool and controlled.

"Hello, Mrs. Henderson. How can I help you?"

"A very expensive piece of jewelry has gone missing from our home. A tennis bracelet worth $10,000."

My heart sank. "I'm so sorry to hear that. When did you notice it was missing?"

"After your team cleaned yesterday. It was in our safe, which was unlocked, and now it's gone."

I found myself in a state of disbelief. The question of why the safe had been left unlocked was one that I felt inappropriate to ask at that time, so it remained a mystery, albeit an inconsequential one. What lay ahead demanded immediate action on my part. This was one of those moments when action, not mere intention, was imperative, for we could not afford to allow our reputation to be tarnished. Admittedly, in the late eighties, the landscape was different, with no Google reviews to concern us. However, our clients were interconnected, and words of a disgruntled client's experience could spread like wildfire in the wrong direction. We needed to prevent this domino effect. There was also the little matter of replacing the $10,000 bracelet. Moreover, ethical considerations guided us to do what was right in this situation. If one of our employees were indeed responsible, it was our responsibility to address it.

"Mrs. Henderson, have any other service providers been in your home recently? Plumbers, electricians, anyone else?"

"No. Just your cleaning team."

"I understand. I'm going to investigate this immediately and get back to you today."

I advised the client to inquire if any other vendors had been in her home, but she remained steadfast in her belief that our cleaning team was responsible. I took it upon myself to question all employees who had visited the client's home. Predictably, none of my employees admitted any wrongdoing. I, of course, believed them. They did, after all, work for me and replicated my values and actions. However, lessons learned at MCI did loom in my head, and the client's conviction that we were culpable persisted.

In my quest for a solution, I turned to a tool frequently employed in detective serials on television during that era, the polygraph test. The widespread use of DNA for investigative purposes had yet to materialize; hence, polygraph examinations were a common method used in criminal investigations to help determine credibility.

This was long before the convenience of Internet searches, so I pulled out the Yellow Pages and began calling polygraph examiners. I left several messages, but only one examiner returned my call and expressed a willingness to discuss the situation.

During that conversation, I learned something that surprised me. Using a polygraph on private employees had been made illegal by Congress years earlier, with one major exception: government agencies were still allowed to use them. The reason for the law, as had been explained to him, was that polygraphs had begun to be misused by some corporations during the hiring process. Instead of focusing on job-related integrity issues, certain employers and executives were asking deeply personal and inappropriate questions. In response, Congress stepped in and sharply restricted their use in the private sector.

The examiner I ultimately worked with had a background that underscored how seriously he took the tool. In addition to private investigative work, he conducted postconviction polygraph testing for violent offenders in the criminal justice system as part of risk and supervision evaluations before they were released back into the community. His experience in that setting gave him a strong belief in the value of polygraphs as a behavioral and accountability tool, even within the legal limitations surrounding their use.

Although the legal boundaries made the situation complicated, his willingness to help came from a firm conviction that polygraph examinations, when used appropriately, could bring clarity to situations clouded by suspicion, conflicting stories, and damaged trust.

With cautious optimism, I arranged for a polygraph test with the examiner. My choice of the employee to be tested was based on logical reasoning: the most recent hire. Before she joined the team, there were no prior issues. She was a dedicated and trustworthy worker, qualities that had endeared her to me.

In accordance with the polygraph test's protocol, I invited her into my office and disclosed my intentions.

"Please, sit down," I said, gesturing to the chair across from my desk.

She sat nervously. "Is everything okay?"

"I need to talk to you about something serious. As you know, one of our clients is missing a very expensive bracelet. A $10,000 tennis bracelet."

Her eyes widened. "I didn't take anything!"

"I believe you," I said carefully. "But here's the situation. The client is convinced someone from our team took it. To clear this up and protect everyone, I'm asking if you'd be willing to take a polygraph test."

"A lie detector test?"

"Yes. If you cooperate and tell the truth, the police won't need to be involved. If you refuse or if you fail the test, then I'll have no choice but to call them."

She was quiet for a moment, then nodded. "Okay. I'll do it. I have nothing to hide."

If she cooperated and told the truth, I assured her that the police need not be involved. I explained the polygraph test's requirement and emphasized that failure to pass would lead to police intervention. She adamantly denied any involvement in the theft, and her sincerity resonated with me. One procedural step for the polygraph test was obtaining a signed letter of consent from the employee. Additionally, a waiting period of forty-eight hours was mandated before the test could take place. Not wanting to allow this "possible thief" into another client's home meant that the employee would not be able to earn a paycheck during this time. To provide support and assurance, I offered her office tasks to mitigate the financial impact. As I spent more time with her, I became increasingly convinced of her innocence.

The day of the polygraph test arrived, and she appeared at the office, our residence punctually. Accompanying her to the test, I observed the process unfolded, beginning with a comprehensive review of the test questions. Following this, the examiner affixed straps to her arms, positioning her in a wooden chair reminiscent of a lawn chair. I left the examination room as they deliberated on the questions, returning to my office where I anxiously awaited the examiner's call. He had promised to contact me once the test concluded.

Approximately an hour later, the phone rang, and it was the polygraph examiner on the line.

"Sharon, I've got the results."

"And?"

"Do you want to come and pick up the bracelet, or should I bring it to you?"

I was stunned into silence.

"Sharon? Are you there?"

"She…she had it?"

"Yes. She failed the test. When I confronted her, she pulled it out of her purse."

It seemed she had hoped to pass the test and only relinquished the stolen item upon realizing her failure, fearing that the involvement of the police was imminent. I promptly informed the client of these developments, though they ultimately chose not to pursue legal action. Since the bracelet hadn't been stolen from me, I lacked the grounds to press charges. A second lesson learned about employee truth and integrity.

Remarkably, despite these circumstances, our clients stood by our side. They knew that if any issues arose, we would handle them responsibly and conscientiously. Though these clients were aware that such incidents could happen with any home-service business, they appreciated our commitment to resolution and support.

On select occasions, if a client suspected theft and had connections within the police department, the police themselves would administer and finance the polygraph test for the accused. This scenario unfolded just once in my experience when an attorney with unwavering convictions believed one of our cleaners had stolen items from his home. He initially approached the situation with a sense of superiority, treating me as if I were oblivious to life's intricacies, let alone running a business. In this instance,

I initially held strong reservations about accusing the cleaner in question. However, my rational side prevailed, and I ensured that she underwent the polygraph test. As I predicted, she passed the test with flying colors. The police department promptly conveyed the outcome to the attorney. The attorney called me that afternoon. His tone was completely different.

"Ms. Butza, I owe you and your employee a sincere apology."

"I appreciate that," I said, genuinely surprised.

"I may have damaged her self-esteem by putting her through this ordeal. I feel terrible about it."

"She's a strong person. She understood why it had to be done."

"Still, I'm sorry. And I want you to know, I've referred three of my colleagues to your service. You handled this with such professionalism."

To my astonishment, he exhibited a complete reversal of demeanor. He expressed concern that he may have exacerbated her self-esteem issues. I accepted his apology graciously, never expecting what transpired next. Over the following month, we did acquire three new repeat clients that were referred by this attorney.

The reliability of polygraph tests was further validated in our experiences as we encountered theft cases. Each time, I accurately identified the suspect within the team, eliminating the need to test the remaining individuals. While this spared us the expense of multiple tests, it also ensured that the guilty party could not return to work. Subsequently, the police departments collaborated with us and the affected clients to recover the stolen items and, hopefully, apprehend the thief.

One incident demonstrated the dedication of a client who tenaciously pursued answers. Although the police initially failed to locate the stolen jewelry in local pawnshops, to satisfy my client's beliefs, I followed through with polygraphing my most recent hire on the team. The cleaner failed the test. We notified the police department and subsequent efforts to check the pawnshops successfully recovered all the stolen items. Through these challenging circumstances, we retained the trust and loyalty of our clients. They knew that we were a company that would never leave them without an accurate explanation and full restoration. Even when the police gave up, we did not, only to find out we were guilty. Then we did everything we could to return our client's lives to the way they were before this happened.

In our 20 years in business, cleaning 495 homes per week, we were involved in nine theft suspicions. We were guilty in three. In the quest to assemble a dependable and trustworthy team, I ventured into the realm of employee assessments. These evaluations purported to reveal an individual's honesty and suitability for long-term employment, traits I considered paramount in our search for the ideal cleaner. For a period, we implemented the Stanton survey, albeit for a brief six-month stint. My hopes were pinned on this tool to help us steer clear of any potential thieves and our commitment to excellence left no room for compromise. The Stanton survey came at a significant cost, especially given the technology limitations of the era. Back then, everything operated on paper, and the surveys had to be physically mailed to us, arriving in batches of five, ten, fifteen, and so forth. The more we purchased, the more economical they became, yet it still translated to a considerable investment. If memory serves, each survey for an employee cost $15, a price tag that would equate to $35 in today's currency. With such an expenditure, I held high expectations for remarkable results.

By this juncture, our financial standing allowed us to explore more costly solutions that promised to streamline our business processes. In my pursuit of improvement, I maintained an open-minded approach, willing to experiment with new methods. The application of the Stanton survey, however, proved to be time-consuming and occasionally provided results that contradicted my own assessments of prospective hires. Despite my initial inclination to trust my instincts, I resolved to adhere to the survey results to ensure a fair evaluation process. We all know I made some hiring mistakes. After all, why invest in a tool if I intended to override its outcomes based solely on my gut feeling?

At that time, a dedicated and highly skilled member of our team, Manuel, who had worked with us for four years, regrettably had to leave the company and return to Mexico. His position was far more valuable than the job title suggested. On paper, he cleaned windows and screens inside and out, steam cleaned carpets, power washed exteriors, and towed broken-down company vehicles using our Ramcharger, trailer, and winch. In reality, he was one of the most financially strategic people in our entire operation.

Because we ran older company cars, breakdowns and fender benders were simply part of life. Thankfully, no one was ever seriously injured in any of our accidents, but tow trucks always circled like vultures the moment a car stalled or got hit. And then, like clockwork, here came The Upstairs Maid Ramcharger, an SUV with a covered trailer, pulling up like we were part of the rescue crew. Manuel would calmly back up, get out his winch, hook up the vehicle, load it onto the trailer, and haul it to our mechanic out in the country.

That one capability saved us thousands upon thousands of dollars in towing fees over the years. For smaller cities or rural operations, having someone like that on your team is gold. When a vehicle couldn't be repaired, our mechanics salvaged usable parts, doors, handles, trim, and stored them behind the shop in what they jokingly called the precious-metals yard. It wasn't glamorous, but it was incredibly effective.

Running a fleet also taught me another lesson: Standardization reduces chaos. We tried to keep all cars the same make and model, usually small white Geo Metros, because familiarity reduces accidents. Southwest Airlines flies the same planes. UPS drivers use the same trucks and make mostly right-hand turns. Consistency lowers error rates. When a cleaner had to switch cars in the dark, in the rain, or in a rush, they already knew where everything was. That matters more than people realize.

One Thanksgiving season, Colleen had two accidents within thirty days, neither her fault. The first damaged one side of her white Geo Metro. Our mechanics only had a red door available, so it went. Two weeks later, she got hit again on the opposite side. This time the only replacement door was green. The car came back red, white, and green just in time for Christmas. Colleen put a wreath on the front grille and proudly drove what became known as the Christmas Car. Customers called asking when the Christmas car would arrive. It was ridiculous, and unforgettable. Sometimes personality does more marketing than money ever could.

But Manuel's value didn't stop at saving money. He generated revenue. With a large base of repeat clients, there were always windows to wash and carpets to clean. If his schedule ever opened, we simply reviewed our client list and called homes that had dirty windows or carpets to offer a "special opening." He stayed busy, and his overtime paid for itself many times over.

When we were short on cleaners, Manuel went into the field and cleaned bathrooms. Specialty work like windows and carpets could be moved. Repeat house cleanings could not. If we wanted to keep clients on a recurring schedule, those homes had to be cleaned first, no matter what. "The cows must be milked" always rings in my ears. No matter what.

That's where flexibility came in. If Manuel had window jobs scheduled but we needed him on a cleaning team, we adjusted. On bright sunny days, we would call the window clients and explain that direct sunlight makes it nearly impossible to see streaks properly and ask if they'd prefer to reschedule for a better day. Most appreciated the honesty. On overcast days, we might say the opposite, that a sunny day would give them better results. We did the same with carpet jobs, watching humidity and drying conditions.

The point wasn't excuses. The point was priorities. Repeat maintenance cleaning protected the relationship and the recurring revenue. Specialty services were important, but they had flexibility built in. Manuel understood that, and because he did, we were able to protect our core business while still generating additional income when the timing was right.

Manuel was trusted like family. Competent, dependable, flexible, honest, he embodied everything we valued. When employees called with unusual problems, our answer was simple: "Call Manuel." Losing him wasn't just losing a technician. It was losing a stabilizer in both our operations and our finances.

His departure created a void that was nearly impossible to fill, because what made him valuable wasn't just skill. It was versatility, ownership, and the willingness to do whatever the business needed that day.

After conducting interviews and subjecting all candidates to the Stanton survey, I ultimately selected Javier. Javier's results on the Stanton survey were exemplary, aligning with our expectations. Moreover, his background check revealed no prior arrests within our county records, and he possessed a degree of experience relevant to the responsibilities of the role. Manual had the opportunity to impart his knowledge to Javier before his departure, allowing Javier to acclimate to his new position within a week. He exceeded our expectations, receiving favorable reviews from clients and fulfilling our requirements admirably. Approximately two and a half months into his employment, Javier failed to show up for work and did not call us. And we could not reach him on the phone or in a text. A palpable sense of disbelief washed over us as our attempts to contact him or his designated emergency contact went unanswered.

As the second day unfolded with no sign of Javier, we recognized the need to involve the police department, evoking memories of my MCI days. To our surprise, the police department introduced us to yet another startling revelation: When a company entrusts an employee with a company vehicle, the law stipulates that a report of a stolen vehicle cannot be filed until forty-eight hours after the vehicle's disappearance. This revelation left me incredulous, for I foresaw that delaying a report might result in the vehicle being disassembled and transported to Mexico, a lucrative destination for a vehicle like our Ramcharger. The vehicle had originally belonged to Mike when we initiated the company, but with the expansion of our services, we integrated it into our fleet, providing us with no recourse but to trust the individuals we assigned these vehicles to. My decision to invest significant sums in the Stanton surveys had been based on a desire to mitigate such risks, but the current situation revealed its shortcomings.

On the third day of Javier's absence, the police department initiated their investigative efforts by checking pawnshops, suspecting that Javier may have pawned our equipment for financial gain. Their suspicions proved accurate when we received a call from a pawnshop later that afternoon, reporting the presence of our Durango in their parking lot, supported by a disheartening sight of the vehicle elevated on cement blocks, bereft of its tires. Prior to abandoning the vehicle, Javier had pawned various items, including the steam cleaner, at this very establishment. It was a bewildering turn of events.

I disposed of the Stanton surveys, returning to the reliance on my instincts and comprehensive background checks. I expanded the scope of these background checks, extending beyond our county to encompass the entire state. The police informed me that this alteration would have flagged Javier, who had prior theft-related incidents on record in Corpus Christi. It provided an added layer of protection against potential thieves. Regrettably, this episode served as a stark reminder that, at times, the price of conducting business in this industry involves navigating unexpected challenges and, ultimately, learning from them. There is no such thing as a magic wand that will protect you from all damaging circumstances. I thought I had the magic wand with the Stanton surveys that said Javier was an honest man who would never steel anything. Not a very magic wand.

CHAPTER 12

MANAGING TEAM PLAYERS

Employees have always been a mystery to me. I've always believed that hiring should be done by the person to whom the new hire directly reports. I walked away from a very good, powerful, high-paying job over that principle.

One of my seventeen jobs was working in the billing department for Froedtert Hospital. I had eighty ladies reporting to me. At that time, they were all women. We were still doing tape-to-tape billing. Every month we sent a huge reel to Medicaid, Medicare, and the major insurance companies with all of our invoices for each patient.

We billed a couple of million dollars a month back then, with charges that ran as little as ten cents for a Band-Aid to $1,200 for the operating room. Whatever items or services were used during a patient's stay, or as an outpatient, were billed by our facility, Faculty Health Services (FHS).

It was a big job, but I had an excellent mentor, and I was a fast learner. I took away a couple of career life lessons from that job.

The manager I replaced at FHS was loved by everybody, employees, managers, VPs, and doctors. The only reason he was leaving was because he had embezzled a lot of funds. As usual, the hospital did not press charges. That's standard in the corporate world, and in this case, it would have been especially difficult. Everyone adored him. Pressing charges would have crushed morale, even though he had committed a crime.

The search for his replacement took ninety days. During that time, they let him keep doing the job and even gave him time to train me once they chose me. Crazy. I can see why everyone liked him though. He really was a great guy, which left me with some rather large boots to fill.

This was the very first real management job I ever had. I had coached phone solicitors before, but I wasn't their manager. I didn't hire them, and I couldn't fire them. I trained staff at nursing home facilities during the decentralization of billing, but again, I wasn't their boss. I was sort of a corporate consultant.

Now, suddenly, I was going to manage eighty people who already knew what they were doing, and I had no idea what I was doing. I landed that job the way I landed a lot of things in my life: through one of those wonderful "breaks" people like to call good luck. I agree with that term if your definition of good luck is "where hard work and opportunity cross."

I was nervous and clueless. But I received some wonderful advice from the man whose shoes I could never fill. One of the first things he taught me was about managing people, especially large staff. It's something I've never forgotten, and I was fortunate to learn it in my very first management job.

He said, "Sharon, there is no way that all of these people will like you. That's just not going to happen, so don't even try. But what better be true is that they all respect you."

I have carried that advice with me through all the years I've been managing people.

I believe that God gives everyone some special talents, something they do far better than the average person. I believe God gave me the ability to work with employees, especially entry-level employees. I was gifted with the ability to motivate, encourage, educate, and uplift employees at every level.

I am extremely patient with my employees. Not so much with owners.

A big part of my rapport with employees is something very simple: helping them see that there is something better for them out there and then helping them set goals to reach it. I wanted them to see our company as a steppingstone, not just a job they could get stuck in for the rest of their lives in a world full of people trying to take advantage of them.

I helped them find their next steppingstone, the next place they needed to go to get where they wanted to go. Many employees at this level don't have a clue where they want to go. They've never even thought about an alternative to where they are.

Had they not come to our company, many of them probably would have cleaned houses the rest of their lives. Some of our cleaners, thankfully, wanted to do nothing more than clean homes for the remainder of their working years, and when that was true, we left them alone. We honored that. But for those who wanted more from their careers, we helped them pursue more. And if they were satisfied with cleaning forever, we still helped them find another goal, often something related to their children's advancement. With the close family ties in the Hispanic culture, that was a very common theme. Another very worthy goal. We didn't judge; we just guided, regardless of race, color, or creed.

I lost some of this ability to help my employees excel when I started hiring non-English-speaking cleaners. I had studied Spanish in junior high and high school, so I thought I had some rudimentary skills and would be able to communicate with my new employees to some extent. Ana would interpret for me, but I often felt like something was being lost in translation. Because I couldn't understand what she was saying, I couldn't figure out why what I was trying to convey wasn't landing the way it used to. I didn't see the motivation or change in behavior that I was used to seeing.

I was coaching through Ana. To her credit, Ana had been with us a couple of years, and her English had improved massively in our English-only environment. By then she knew my personality, knew what I was trying to get across, and she also knew that if someone's behavior didn't change, they wouldn't be working with us much longer.

Ana was sympathetic, great at relating to people, and a strong advocate for the cleaners. If there was something she felt I wasn't hearing on behalf of a cleaner, she made sure to bring it to my attention.

Eventually, that horrible day came. Another complaint came in about the inferior quality of work performed by a cleaner who was already on probation and had signed paperwork acknowledging that the next step was termination, or so I thought.

We really had no choice but to terminate her. I felt like a failure, and I suspect she felt it came out of nowhere, even though we had sat with her three different times and had her sign documents.

I knew something had gone wrong because I had never had a dismissed cleaner cry when I terminated them. They usually knew it was coming. They'd received three notices and still refused to change their behavior.

Whenever I sensed we were about to lose a cleaner because of poor quality, not attendance or attitude, but quality, my patience would kick in; and I would spend the time, money, and attention to be sure they thoroughly understood what had to be cleaned and how to clean it.

I could patiently work with an autistic cleaner until they could follow the process exactly. It warmed my heart to see the prideful smile spread across their face when they'd say, "Look, look. I remembered. I love this system." At that moment, I also knew I had a "lifer" for an employee.

Back then there weren't many applicants who openly shared that they were autistic. Either there weren't as many diagnosed or they were afraid that sharing that information would hurt their chances of being hired. Today there's an ever-increasing percentage of people entering the workforce who are challenged by autism, and many share that information at the interview or by the end of their first day of training. Cleaning homes is a perfect job for many of them, if you are using a tight, step-driven process to clean.

On the flip side, I had absolutely no patience with someone who refused to follow directions once they understood them. If I had taken extra time to ensure an employee was fully trained and understood what was expected, I had no problem dismissing them if they were simply lazy or stubborn and refused to follow our process.

I'm sure those employees weren't very fond of me when they left, but I do believe they respected me. Some of them even told me that. A lot of them wanted to return to work shortly after being terminated.

It would have been much easier to just ignore a cleaner's problems and hope they'd go away with enough insults, horrible workdays, or reduced hours. But what would that accomplish for either one of us? There's always the possibility that if you clearly acknowledge the problem, they will fix it. I would estimate that about 70 percent of the employees who received a first verbal warning had no idea how serious the problem was until we confronted them with it.

As I watched the tears stream down this cleaner's face, I realized she had received none of the coaching I was used to providing. She probably came to me with little or no self-esteem, as most entry-level cleaners do, or they wouldn't be cleaning houses for a living. Yes, some cleaners love this work and enter the field by design, but then they usually become self-employed solo cleaners.

Those tears tugged at my heart for the rest of the day. On the way home, I questioned my own integrity and principles, feeling like I was abusing this new group of non-English-speaking cleaners. My only concern for them was how many hours they could work each day.

My God-given blessing is to help others raise their self-esteem, and here I was essentially telling this cleaner that she couldn't even clean toilets.

No, that wasn't entirely true. The real problem was that I couldn't tell her anything in a language she understood, nor could I be sure anyone else was teaching her correctly.

The words of wisdom from that FHS manager began ringing in my ears. How could these new hires respect me? They couldn't even understand me. How could I truly respect them if I couldn't understand them? I could be sitting on unbelievable talent and not know it.

I clearly had a problem to fix, and it needed to be fixed yesterday. As was my MO when I had an inconvenient situation, I called my mother.

I had contacted Austin Community College earlier that afternoon, but they needed proof of successful completion of my BA before they would let me into classes without testing. Ironically, my mom still had my college degree.

"Mom, I need a favor," I said when she answered.

"Of course. What is it?"

"Remember my college degree? The one you've been keeping all these years?"

"Yes, it's in the attic. Why?"

"I need you to mail it to me. I'm going back to school."

There was a pause, then excitement in her voice. "Really? For what?"

"Spanish classes. I need to learn Spanish so I can communicate with my employees."

"Oh, Sharon, that's wonderful! Your father and I have always hoped you'd value that education more."

She was thrilled that I was finally asking for it. She and Dad had paid for it, and I think it always broke their hearts that I didn't value it more. They were wrong about that. I never would have left Watertown and built the life I have without that BA.

I had decided to add one more overwhelming task to my already impossible daily to-do list: I was going back to school to learn Spanish, for credit.

I am an overachiever. If I'm being watched or scored, I'll usually end up near the top. But if there's no structure and no accountability, my effort drops fast. That's exactly what happened with French in college. I learned just enough to earn the BA I wanted at the time, but not enough to actually use the language. In fact, it erased most of the Spanish I had learned earlier.

This time was different. I didn't need a grade; I needed results. I needed to speak and understand Spanish well enough to communicate with my team. That meant consistency, not cramming. It meant daily repetition, not last-minute effort. Over time, those small, steady sessions built real ability. After sixteen credits, I was functioning at about 70 percent fluency, not perfect but practical.

That experience reinforced something I would later see again and again in business: real skill comes from repeatable effort, not bursts of intensity. Fluency, like clean homes and strong teams, is built through consistent practice that compounds over time.

Today I train cleaners all over the world who don't speak a word of English, and I know firsthand what it takes to bridge that gap.

I made it well known throughout our company that I was taking Spanish classes. I wanted everyone to know I was taking a step to bridge the gap between myself and our non-English-speaking cleaners. I wanted to be able to resolve issues by understanding both sides.

The non-English speakers were thrilled. For once in their lives, they were working for someone who was going to learn their language, instead of shouting at them for not knowing English.

Their gratitude didn't get them off the hook though. From that day forward, anyone who couldn't speak English had to learn five English words per week if they wanted to work for The Upstairs Maid. If they didn't learn them, they couldn't get their paycheck.

Of course, we all know that's not legal, but they didn't know that. I will admit that could be viewed as exploitation, but there is sometimes a fine line between exploitation and forced education.

Announcing that I was learning Spanish and that everyone else was learning English created a paradigm shift that transformed our company from "near shutdown" only six months earlier to enviable growth and structure from that day forward.

Eventually, I realized it was time to put another manager in place. Keri couldn't speak Spanish. I learned on the first day of my Spanish class that I also could not speak Spanish, at least not grammatically.

I was learning Spanish as fast as I could, but we were overwhelmed trying to handle everyone who couldn't speak English. Ana and our bilingual supervisor helped tremendously, but I knew it was time for someone else to take some teams off my plate so I could spend more time developing managers.

I am a strong advocate of promoting from within, especially if you are a small company. There are very few higher-level positions available, and I didn't want to fill them from the outside. People from outside our company didn't really understand our business anyway.

I posted the field operations manager position internally to all our current cleaners. All the supervisors filled out the posting form. Everyone was excited about their interview. That part actually backfired. They all asked for fewer jobs the day of their interview so they could go home, shower, and get dressed up. They all showed up on time, looked fabulous, did the best they could, and walked out thinking they were the one who would get the job.

That's the problem with internal postings. You owe each candidate a valid explanation if they don't get the promotion, or you risk losing supervisors and future leaders.

Some people in an organization simply aren't management material, and it's hard to articulate why. Many of them had been there a long time and felt that longevity automatically qualified them. I had a couple of those people. Peggy Bailey was the first.

Peggy was extremely likeable, and the clients adored her. She loved it when we went to three-person teams because she managed to put herself in an area with less work, allowing for more time to chat with clients.

Peggy was also a functional alcoholic.

She had a college degree in teaching, but she'd had so many DUIs that she couldn't get a teaching position. Maybe today she could, but not in the early nineties. She rarely missed work. She was just hung over every day.

After a few months, Peggy brought her husband, Ted, in for an interview. Like Peggy, he was an alcoholic, but not nearly as healthy. He had a high school degree and some serious health and drinking issues, but he also never missed work.

Ted was a nice guy. Not as engaging or intelligent as Peggy, but very polite. His biggest drawback was the fact that he did not do practical things like brushing his teeth each morning after drinking a case of beer the night before.

Peggy and Ted both became supervisors. I really loved them both. This was also a time when many clients did not want a male cleaner in their home, but Ted pulled it off. He had a driver's license, as did Peggy. I'm still not sure how, but somehow, they managed to keep getting them back after each DUI.

Peggy found the supervisor's position easy and "palatable." Both she and Ted loved positioning themselves in the kitchen. Supervisors were supposed to do the dusting, but whenever possible Peggy would put herself in the kitchen, and so would Ted.

Most kitchens are the cleanest room in the home. If someone is willing to take money out of their budget to pay someone to keep their home free of dust, dirt, and grime, chances are they're not going to bed with a filthy kitchen after dinner. You can, however, make it look to the rest of your team like the kitchen is the dirtiest, most time-consuming room in the home.

Alcoholics like Peggy and Ted were experts at this. They went through a lot of partners, because the partners ended up cleaning the majority of the home while Peggy and Ted "hid" in the kitchen.

Both were with us for about ten years, and I never really pushed the issue.

Then Peggy posted for the manager position. A woman who had been with me for ten years, had a college degree, clients loved her, and she stood beside me through the Dell mutiny.

How could I not promote her without making her feel like there was no future for her in our company? The truth was, there really wasn't. But I decided to try something. I allowed all supervisors who posted for the manager's position to take that job for a three-day test run.

I've never been a big fan of trial runs for applicants. I don't think it's fair to them. But in this case, it felt like the right move, and it was.

One candidate decided after one day that she wanted nothing to do with the position. After each day, I met with the trainees to get feedback on their experience.

Peggy's first trainee came back with an interesting report.

"How did it go?" I asked.

The trainee hesitated. "Well…it was good—in the afternoon."

"What about the morning?"

"She told me as soon as we got in the car that she doesn't like mornings and prefers not to chat before noon."

I raised my eyebrows. "She said that?"

"Yes. She said if I understood that, we'd get along just fine. So we didn't talk all morning. I didn't get any training until after lunch."

"And the afternoon?"

"Oh, the afternoon was great! She's a really good trainer. She taught me everything I needed to know."

So sad, but I knew immediately that Peggy could not spend another day training.

Now what?

I had promised her there would be a future for her beyond cleaning and supervising. The truth was, there wasn't. So where were my integrity and principles now?

Exactly where they'd always been. I needed to help Peggy improve her life.

I called one of my fellow members from American Business Women's Association, Nancy, who worked at a temp agency.

"Nancy, I need your help. I have an employee who's incredibly talented but not quite right for the management position I'm trying to fill."

"Tell me about her."

"Her name's Peggy. She's smart, clients love her, she's been with me for ten years. But she's a functional alcoholic and mornings are…difficult."

Nancy laughed. "Say no more. I might have the perfect thing. HEB is looking for a bakery manager. The shift starts at 1:00 p.m."

"Really?"

"Yes. She'd have three people reporting to her, good benefits after ninety days, and more pay than you're offering. Want me to set up an interview?"

"Nancy, you're a lifesaver."

I sat down with Peggy the next day.

"Peggy, I want to talk to you about something. I know your planning on the field operations manager position, and I want you to know you're an incredible employee."

She smiled, but I could see the nervousness in her eyes.

"However, I don't think that position is the right fit for you. But I found something that might be even better."

I told her about the HEB opportunity, the afternoon start time, the benefits, the pay increase.

Her eyes lit up. "That sounds perfect actually."

"I thought it might be. Nancy at the temp agency is expecting your call."

She interviewed with HEB, got the job, turned in her resignation; and we had an amazing going-away party for her. Ted continued to work for us until I left the company.

Peggy and Ted respected me, and I respected them. I believe we were all grateful for what we had added to each other's lives.

The second "problem" posting for the field manager position was Chris Farrell. I don't know exactly why, but I just felt she wasn't the right person for this very difficult operation's role.

She had been with us a long time. She waited sixteen months to become a supervisor. If longevity alone qualified someone for promotion, then Chris would have been first in line.

The feedback from her trial days as manager, however, was lukewarm at best. The trainees weren't exactly inspired. Once again, I turned to Nancy at the temp agency.

Nancy found Chris a great job, traveling around the country, training people on how to use fax machines and similar equipment. Chris was a great trainer, but she wasn't management material, and I needed both.

I was pleased with how things turned out for both Chris and Peggy, but my need for an operations manager still hadn't been resolved.

Around that time, I started hiring some very talented bilingual cleaners. One of them, Luis, came with a lot of management experience working with Hispanic crews. He was intelligent, extremely good-looking, polished, and spoke both English and Spanish perfectly.

I promoted him to the management position in two weeks.

After that, the shift clearly happened. Though we didn't plan it that way, we only hired one non-Latino cleaner after that. The applicants who walked in our door were primarily Hispanic, Brazilian, and Colombian, referred by family and friends. We weren't trying to profile; we simply hired the people who came to us and fit our standards.

I continued our referral bonuses, $50 for a cleaner and $250 for a driving working supervisor, both paid on the new hire's ninetieth day. This was a lot of money to a Hispanic family.

The only non-Latino employee we had at that point was Ted, until Colleen called one day sounding very remorseful.

"Sharon? It's Colleen."

I was surprised to hear her voice. "Colleen! How are you?"

"Not great, actually. I got laid off from Dell."

"Oh no. I'm so sorry."

"They moved a big part of the factory operation to Arkansas. All the temps got cut first. No benefits, so we were easy to let go." There was a pause. "Sharon, I know I don't deserve it, but…would you consider taking me back?"

I thought about what she had done to our company: the mass exodus, the chaos, the near collapse.

But I also thought about her work ethic, her dedication, her ability to get things done.

"Colleen, you know things have changed here, right? We're mostly Hispanic cleaners now. Very few speak English."

"I don't care who I work with as long as I can get back to work. Please, Sharon. I trust you. I don't want to work for anyone else."

I explained the paradigm shift our company had gone through. I couldn't find English-speaking employees anymore. Even though Michael Dell had left town, a lot of other high-tech companies had moved in. Unemployment was now 1.9 percent, and I don't think it ever got much better, for employers.

"I only have two cars available right now," I continued. "One has to stay as a spare. The only car you could drive is a standard transmission with a stick shift."

"I know how to drive stick! That'll be fun!"

I hired Colleen back, and she started the following Monday. Luis told me he had two cleaners ready to start, so I told him I needed them Monday as Colleen's partners. Neither of them spoke English, and Colleen didn't speak a word of Spanish.

One of those women was Colleen's partner the entire time I remained with the company. The other partnered with her for seven years until she tragically died one Christmas. Colleen then took on a new partner, and that partner also stayed until I left.

Colleen's partners truly respected her. Not just liked her, respected her. There is no way they would have been such exemplary employees if they hadn't been directed by Colleen.

I continued teaching English words, holding quarterly developmental retreats on Saturdays, and running monthly informative and educational meetings. Luis, my new manager, handled the one-on-ones while I increased my networking efforts. I was, after all, the face of the company and the lead generator.

I had a wealth of employees, and Austin continued to offer us a steady stream of clients.

Why would I change anything?

Well…maybe one thing. But that's the next story.

Because as stable as we looked from the outside, I kept seeing something that didn't add up on the inside. Two people could start at the same time, get the same training, work in the same types of homes, and still have completely different outcomes. One would be thriving a year later, the kind of employee who could train others and hold the culture together. The other would disappear in a few weeks, sometimes without warning, sometimes after one small disappointment that shouldn't have mattered as much as it did.

That's when I realized managing team players wasn't only about hiring and coaching. It was about understanding what makes people stay, what bonds a group together, and why some teams become loyal and unstoppable while others never turn into anything real. I didn't have language for it yet, but once I did, it changed the way I structured everything.

CHAPTER 13

GROWING A TEAM THAT WANTS TO STAY

At some point during our growth, when we had moved beyond a handful of part-time cleaners and were starting to manage real teams in real homes every day, I was introduced to a framework that would eventually explain more about turnover, retention, and leadership than any hiring system or pay scale ever had.

It came from a gentleman named LaCoursierre, who had been studying how teams grow together over time and why some groups of people move forward collectively while others, given the same leadership and the same goals, never quite seem to gel. Later, Steven Rowel, who had worked with Disney and eventually wrote *Clean Is Not Enough*, adapted LaCoursierre's concepts specifically to the residential cleaning industry.

At the time, I didn't think I needed a framework to tell me how teams worked. We were hiring, orienting, assigning partners, and sending people into the field every day. From the outside, it looked straightforward enough. But something wasn't adding up.

Two employees could start on the same day, receive the same orientation, clean the same types of homes, and spend their days doing the same work under different supervisors. One would still be with us two years later, helping train others. The other would be gone in a matter of weeks.

It didn't always make sense. Sometimes the one who left was faster. Sometimes the one who stayed wasn't. It wasn't always about skill, and it certainly wasn't always about pay.

LaCoursierre's work described something we were already seeing but didn't yet have language for. According to his model, teams don't simply form because you assign people to work together. They grow through five stages: safety, trust, intimacy, goals and tasks, and, finally, mission.

I began watching our own teams through that lens.

On a new employee's first day, they are not thinking about quality or efficiency. They are thinking about themselves. Who are these people? Do they like me? Where do I sit in the car? Am I allowed to bring my purse into the house? What happens if I fall behind? When do we eat lunch?

I remember one new cleaner whose last hundred dollars for groceries was sitting in her purse in the company car while we were inside a client's home. That money was for her family's dinner that night. While the rest of the team was focused on cleaning, she was focused on whether someone might break into the car. She wasn't distracted because she didn't care about her job. She was distracted because she didn't yet feel safe.

LaCoursierre called this the safety stage.

Once an employee felt physically and emotionally safe—once someone had introduced themselves, explained what the day would look like, told them where to sit, and assured them that they wouldn't be left alone in a bathroom with no help—they could begin to move into the second stage: trust.

Trust didn't come from an orientation or a policy manual. It came from follow-through. If a supervisor said they would stop for lunch and then didn't, that mattered. If the office promised a new shirt and forgot to order it, that mattered. If a partner said, "We'll help you with that bathroom," and then didn't, that mattered even more.

A promise broken by anyone in the organization didn't set that employee back slightly. It sent them all the way back to safety. It didn't matter whether the supervisor kept their word if the office didn't, or whether the office followed through if the partner didn't. To the new employee, we were one company. One broken promise meant they could no longer trust the system.

But when that trust did begin to build, something subtle started to change. Employees relaxed. They talked between jobs. They asked questions they wouldn't have asked before. They noticed whether their partners liked talking in the morning or preferred quiet. They started bringing breakfast tacos for one another or doughnuts on a Friday morning. One of our supervisors once drove thirty miles out of her way before a 7:30 a.m. start time to pick up tacos for her team because she had heard me talk about small gestures building trust. I'm not sure she needed to drive thirty miles to do it, but she did, and it mattered.

This was intimacy, not in the personal sense but in the comfort of familiarity.

They knew one another's pace. They knew who moved quickly through kitchens and who preferred bathrooms. They laughed between jobs. They shared rides. They knew when someone was having a difficult morning without asking why. It was also at this stage that language began to shift.

Instead of saying "my" team, they began to say "we." Not consciously, but naturally. The job stopped being something they went to for the company and became something they showed up for with each other. And people don't leave jobs nearly as often when they enjoy the people they work with every day.

From there, teams began to move into what LaCoursierre called the goals and tasks stage. Their focus shifted outward. They talked about how to get through a house faster without sacrificing quality. They reminded one another which clients tipped consistently. They vacuumed last not only because it was efficient, but because it gave them a final opportunity to look around the room and catch anything a partner might have missed.

They were protecting one another from callbacks as much as they were protecting the company.

Mistakes weren't hidden. They were corrected quietly because no one wanted a partner to be embarrassed by a redo. If one person was behind, another might grab a bathroom just to keep the day moving. Their work became physically easier because it was shared more evenly and mentally easier because they no longer felt alone in it.

Eventually, for the teams that stayed together long enough, there was mission and vision.

They understood not only what they were doing, but why they were doing it. They began to see advancement paths within the company: supervisor roles, operations management positions, administrative leadership. They weren't just cleaning houses anymore. They were building something that could take them somewhere else inside the organization.

That was where our managers came from.

It was also where I learned how easily progress could be undone. Any time we moved someone from one team to another, even for scheduling convenience, we weren't just changing their work assignment. We were sending them back to safety. It could take eight months to a year for a team to move from safety through trust and into intimacy. Reassigning a partner reset that entire process.

Teams moved through safety and trust more quickly because they were in constant interaction with one another. Solos had no such advantage. If they were trained by someone for two days and then never saw that person again, they had no partner to bond with. Their only connection to the organization became the office, which is why I came to believe so strongly in operations managers. Someone had to check in, to answer questions, to provide that human bridge through the early stages until the cleaner felt safe enough to trust the system on their own.

These same five stages applied not only to cleaners, but to supervisors, managers, and eventually to me. Whenever I skipped safety or trust because someone appeared confident, I eventually had to revisit them anyway.

Understanding that changed the way I structured the entire company.

I maintained an administrative side that handled sales, scheduling, customer service, billing, and client communication.

For continuity, I split the city in half. When a client called in, they were asked what side of the city they lived on and were routed to the person who had sold them their service in the first place. I didn't want a client to have to explain their home, their preferences, or their concerns to someone new every time they called. That consistency supported our teams by reducing unnecessary confusion and callbacks.

At one point, we were running ninety-five jobs a day, and it took two administrative staff members to manage the volume. My responsibility as the owner was to make the phone ring enough for them to do that.

In the field, I eventually had three operations managers, each responsible for approximately eighteen cleaners organized into teams of three. Each team had a supervisor responsible for day-to-day coordination, while the operations manager hired, trained, and evaluated new employees during their first ten days using a structured 360-degree review process.

Once employees were on board, supervisors conducted annual reviews, supported by managers when necessary. This structure made it possible for me to manage the company by working directly with the administrative staff and operations managers rather than needing to intervene with every cleaner.

More importantly, it gave employees somewhere to go.

At the mission stage, they didn't have to leave the company to be promoted. They could become supervisors, operations managers, or move into administrative roles. The five stages didn't simply apply to cleaning teams. They applied to leadership at every level.

And if we skipped one, even with the best of intentions, we would find ourselves back there eventually.

For a while, learning those stages and building around them felt like the answer. It gave me a clearer way to lead, a clearer way to structure the company, and a clearer way to understand why people stayed.

It also did something else: It made me more protective.

When your team is built on trust, you don't just feel responsible for schedules and quality. You feel responsible for lives. You start noticing what your employees carry that you never had to carry: language barriers, fear of paperwork, fear of authority, fear of getting pulled over, fear of doing everything right and still being treated like they don't belong.

And once your company becomes a place where people finally feel safe, you start looking for ways to make them safer.

That's exactly what I tried to do next.

And it's how I walked straight into the biggest scam of my life.

CHAPTER 14

THE GREAT SCAM

By the time we hit our twelfth year in business, about 80 percent of our staff was Hispanic. They were the backbone of our company and honestly the backbone of much of America. People go out to dinner, enjoy spotless homes, admire new buildings, and walk through polished grocery store aisles without ever realizing who's powering all of it. They just assume magic elves show up at night and do the work.

If only they knew the truth. Many of the "elves" are hardworking Hispanic men and women who never complain, save money like Olympic-level squirrels, and show up with more gratitude than any workforce I've ever met. I sometimes think if America had even the slightest idea what these families go through just to live their daily lives, the whole country would be marching in the streets on their behalf.

But back then, like most Americans, I didn't understand the full picture either. I only knew the system was so broken that people who wanted to be legal couldn't become legal and employers who wanted to do everything right had no realistic way to do it. If you followed the rules, you didn't have enough workers. If you didn't, well, you didn't sleep much. And let me tell you, I didn't sleep much.

Those were my ICE nightmare years. I would wake up at 2:00 a.m. in a cold sweat imagining the door flying open and federal agents marching into my office like they were storming the beaches of Normandy. It was always dramatic in my dreams. Lights, sirens, flashlights, the whole bit. Meanwhile in real life, I was just sitting at my desk with a cup of decaf tea trying not to have a stroke.

I coached all of my people regardless of race, color, creed or gender. I mentored them. I taught them English five words at a time. Some days the words were helpful. Other days, they learned phrases like, "Please stop microwaving fish in client's homes." I held meetings; checked on families; worried about who might leave; and prayed no one would file anything resembling a complaint, unemployment, discrimination, you name it.

Before all this, unemployment was my biggest fear. That seems adorable now. "Oh dear, someone might get a small check for a few weeks." What a treat. Compared to the thought of ICE shutting us down, unemployment would've felt like a weekend at a spa.

And through all of it, I genuinely cared for these employees. They were so loyal that if someone had walked into our office with an automatic weapon, I truly don't think one person would have moved. They would've looked at him and said, "Just don't shoot the payroll computer."

They worked like champions. They cleaned Austin's homes. They paid taxes through my company. They were doing everything right, except the one thing the legal system made nearly impossible for them to do. Some of them had been waiting seven years for citizenship. Seven. I have houseplants that don't survive seven days.

And the truth is, I didn't build a mostly Hispanic workforce because I woke up one day and decided I wanted to run a bilingual company. I ended up there the same way I ended up at a lot of turning points in my life: by getting backed into a corner and having to invent my way out. I've already told the story of that pivot and the week that forced it in an earlier chapter, because that week was about growth, employees, and survival.

What matters here is what came after.

Once you have a workforce that depends on you, not just for a paycheck but for stability, dignity, and a chance at something better, you start caring about more than training. You start caring about protection. You start caring about whether the system will swallow them whole and whether you'll get swallowed with them.

By then, my company was doing about $1.1M in revenue. We cleaned about sixty homes a day. We were totally residential. Our billing rates were around twenty-seven or twenty-eight dollars an hour, and we always bid by the job. Minimum wage was $3.35 per hour back then, I started partners at $3.75 an hour, supervisors at $4, and I gave supervisors a company car to take home. They could pick up their partners and go to work. That one benefit alone made recruiting easier for me than it was for a lot of my competitors.

I also learned the hard way that if you are going to employ people who are intimidated by America, intimidated by paperwork, and intimidated by authority, then you have to prove, consistently, that you care about them as much as you care about the money they're going to make for you. They cannot feel you're exploiting them in any way, because if they do, they will not respect you. And respect is where everything begins.

It's hard to convince someone you care about them when you hand them a piece of paper and say, "Sign here," knowing they can't read it. I want you to think about that. How would you feel if someone asked you to sign a document you couldn't understand? You'd refuse. Most Americans would. But these employees are easily intimidated. And if you want respect, you have to help them feel safe.

One of the simplest ways to create safety is to put things in their language: job applications, job descriptions, onboarding forms, policies, training materials, meeting content. You can't build trust while asking people to pretend they understand paperwork they can't read. You can build trust when you give them words and standards they can actually follow.

And when you do that, when you learn enough of their language to show respect, and you teach them enough English to help them grow, you don't just improve your cleaning company; you change their families. They show up at parent-teacher conferences without relying on their children to interpret. They gain respect from their kids and their kids' teachers. And that pride follows them home, and it follows them back to work.

That's why I cared so much. That's why I fought so hard. That's why I lost sleep.

Because once I had a workforce that depended on me, not just for a paycheck but for stability, dignity, and a chance at something better, I wanted to do more than train them. I wanted to protect them.

And that's what led directly to the miracle that showed up in my office one day…and set me up for the biggest scam of my life.

One day, one of my supervisors walked into the office with news that seemed too good to be true.

"Sharon, do you have a minute?"

"Of course, Maria. What's up?"

She sat down, excited. "My husband's boss has someone who helps employees get visa cards. Real ones. Legal work permits."

I looked up from my paperwork. "Visa cards? What do you mean?"

"Like cards that let you work legally. And you can travel back and forth to Mexico to see your family without hiding or crossing the desert."

Now, to be clear, the only Visa cards I understood were the ones that came in my wallet and got me 1.5 percent cash back at Kohl's. But apparently there were other cards that let you work legally and travel back and forth to Mexico to see your family without hiding in a trunk or crossing the desert with nothing but a gallon of water and a dream.

"Who is this person?" I asked.

"His name is Brian. He is helping the lawn service owner my husband works for get visa cards. They all got their visas approved."

Well, that sounded like a miracle. So, of course, I made an appointment with the man.

Brian showed up a few days later, cheerful, confident, and holding a folder thick enough to choke a printer.

"Ms. Butza, thank you for meeting with me," he said, shaking my hand firmly.

"Please call me Sharon. So tell me about these work visas."

He sat down and opened his folder with the flourish of a man who'd done this presentation a hundred times. "It's quite simple. There are work visas available for people with skills needed. As an employer, you can request visas for your employees, up to fifty at a time."

"Fifty?"

"Yes. You write a business case explaining why you need these workers and why American citizens can't fill the positions. Given the shortage of cleaners in Austin, that should be easy."

"And they'd be legal? Completely legal?"

"Absolutely. They'd have work permits, Social Security numbers, everything. They could travel freely to Mexico to visit family."

My heart started racing. This was the answer to everything.

"How much does it cost?"

"My fee is $6,600 total. That covers all the paperwork, filing fees, and processing for up to fifty visas."

I didn't question it. Why? Because I was desperate; tired; and living on hope, luck, and the belief that paperwork could solve anything. My ego also whispered, "You fill out forms better than anyone on earth." And I believed that ego. Paperwork was the one battlefield where I never lost a fight.

"When can we start?" I asked.

"I'll need about half up front to begin the process. Once I have your business case and the employee information, I can file everything within two weeks."

I handed over a check for $3,300 that day.

Word spread through the company faster than a rumor at a beauty salon. Morale shot up to the moon. People hugged me. They cried. They prayed for me. I became St. Sharon of Austin, patron saint of paperwork and impossible dreams.

Maria came running into my office. "Sharon! Sharon! The lawn service got their visas! Six of them! Actual approved visas. The kind with barcodes and stamps and government-looking ink."

I nearly fell out of my chair. "They're approved? Real visas?"

"Yes! My husband saw them. They're going to Mexico next week to get their passports!"

I remember thinking, *If they got six, I'll get fifty. That's just math.*

Five days later, I opened my mailbox and there they were: fifty visas. I nearly fell to my knees. I thought, *God is good. Maybe the government is good too.* That lasted about five days.

We threw a celebration that Friday night. Families brought food. Children ran around. Husbands who worked for the lawn service were packing bags for Mexico. Their appointments at the consulate were scheduled for Monday. It felt like Christmas morning.

As soon as the visas hit my desk, I called Brian. He arrived like a man jogging toward a paycheck, because that's exactly what he was doing.

"Brian, they're here! All fifty visas!"

He walked in, took the stack from me, and flipped through them one by one. "These look perfect. Everything's in order."

"So they can use them right away?"

"Absolutely. They just need to take them to the Mexican consulate and they're all set."

I handed him the final check for $3,300. He looked a little too excited to get that check. That should've been clue no. 1, but hindsight is so smart.

Monday afternoon, two wives called crying. They needed immediate time off. Their husbands were stuck in Mexico. That was clue no. 2.

"Sharon, my husband can't come home," one of them sobbed.

"What? Why not?"

"They won't let him back without a passport. But he can't get a passport without money in the bank."

"What do you mean, money in the bank?"

"Ten thousand dollars. In a savings account. For a whole year."

My blood ran cold. "Ten thousand dollars?"

It turns out, you need more than a visa to leave Mexico. You also need a passport. As I look back on this now, I realize that I've been to Mexico many, many times. At that time, all we needed was a driver's license. Who thought you'd also need a passport? A real passport. And in Mexico, to get a passport, you need the equivalent of $10,000 sitting in a savings account for a full year. Ten. Thousand. Dollars.

These families didn't have $10,000 to sit anywhere for a year. Not to mention, they barely trusted banks enough to put $200 into one overnight much less $10,000. Their money stayed in envelopes, mattresses, and sometimes in the freezer next to the tamales.

We were scammed. Not just scammed, scammed at an Olympic professional level.

I called Brian immediately and demanded he come to my office.

He walked in the next day, cool as a cucumber, as if we were just having a friendly chat.

"Brian, four of lawn service employees are stuck in Mexico because they can't get passports. You never told us about the $10,000 requirement."

He shrugged. "The visas are legitimate. They work in the United States. I did my job."

"Your job? Your job was to help these people become legal! Now they're stranded!"

"I provided work visas. If they can't afford passports, that's not my problem."

I felt my face flush with anger. "You knew this would happen. You knew they couldn't afford passports."

He looked me directly in the eyes and said, "Take me to court."

And then he walked out.

He knew exactly what he was doing. He just figured he'd never get caught because who was I going to complain to? The FBI? ICE? Judge Judy?

Let's be real. I wasn't marching into a courthouse to report Brian. The visas themselves were fine. The problem was, the people who would use them weren't legal. If I'd opened my mouth, the judge would've said, "Ma'am, why don't we start with your situation?" Absolutely not.

So the families of the four men who went to Mexico did what they had always done. They hired coyotes. Again. They handled it themselves because they already knew the drill, which was tragic.

And me? I put those fifty visa cards on the back shelf with all my previous brilliant ideas that didn't pan out. Right next to the failed marketing campaigns and the software that couldn't schedule before 8:00 a.m. in the morning.

We moved on, sadder, wiser, and more aware of how broken this country's immigration system truly is.

I still ask myself why we make it impossible for good people to become legal. In the early 1900s, immigrants came with sponsors. Someone vouched for them. Why can't we do that again? Let people come forward with family sponsors and employer sponsors and become part of the country they already support financially, physically, emotionally, and spiritually.

I'm not taking a political stance. I'm taking a human stance. These are wonderful people who deserve better. Their employers deserve better. America deserves better. If we don't fix this problem, we'll run out of service workers. We'll run out of compassion. And we'll run out of patience for a system that punishes the exact people who keep this country running.

CHAPTER 15

BEWARE OF ATTORNEYS

My first real encounter with attorneys came years before I ever owned a business, at a time when I had very little money. I learned early that attorneys tend to appear when someone is looking for blame, or profit, and I had to decide quickly which side of that line I was willing to stand on.

In 1982, I was living in San Antonio, selling dining club cards on the River Walk, two for the price of one. It was not a glamorous job. It was simply the only job I could find at the time. One of seventeen, if I'm being honest. I was between better chapters, learning lessons whether I wanted to or not.

I had no money. Truly none. My boss paid my rent, let me use the company car, and handed me three hundred dollars a month to live on. Three hundred dollars to eat, dress professionally, and survive. It felt humiliating. It also taught me more about sales, and more about myself, than I realized at the time.

One afternoon, my boss and I were walking across the street near the Alamo on our way to a sales appointment on the River Walk. The walk signal turned green. As I stepped off the curb, a pickup truck barreled toward me. The driver wasn't looking at the road.

I remember flying through the air. I remember thinking, oddly enough, *This must be what it feels like to be a bird.* I remember my arms flapping, instinctively, uselessly. I landed fifteen feet away.

I was thirty-two years old. It was 1982. Women wore dresses and nylons to work, and I was wearing both.

The ambulance arrived quickly. I stood up on my own and walked into it. I felt shaken, but I felt fine. My biggest concern wasn't my body; it was the appointment I was now late for and the runs in my nylons that I could already see spreading like ink.

They wanted to take me to the hospital for tests. I refused. They checked my blood pressure, took my information, and eventually let me go.

My boss and I went straight to the appointment.

When we arrived at the restaurant on the River Walk, I apologized profusely, for being late, for how I looked, for the obvious state of my clothes. The owner stared at me for a moment and then said, "Oh my gosh, you're the woman who just got hit crossing the street."

The news had already traveled up and down the River Walk.

We made the sale.

That night, back in my apartment, the phone rang. Then it rang again. The insurance company. Attorneys who wanted to represent me. The representative for the young man who hit me. Everyone was suddenly very concerned about my well-being.

Apparently, the driver had been looking at a beautiful woman on the sidewalk instead of watching where he was going. At that age, that detail almost felt more insulting than the accident itself.

I could have sued. I knew it. They knew it. I could have claimed back pain. Neck pain. Trauma that hadn't yet surfaced. People did it every day. I could have walked away with twenty or thirty thousand dollars without much effort at all.

Instead, I asked for five hundred dollars. Five hundred dollars to replace my ruined dress and nylons.

At the time, that money felt enormous, nearly a month and a half of my income. It would have helped. It would have mattered. But it would have been honest.

I knew how lucky I was. I had seen what happens when luck runs out.

A close family friend's cousin was hit crossing the street on the very same day. She never walked away. She spent a decade in a coma and never truly came back. She has since passed away. That reality was never lost on me.

I had been thrown into the air and walked away the same day.

Integrity, to me, has always been tied to truth. Not what you can get away with. Not what the system allows. Truth.

I could not pretend to be injured when I wasn't. I could not manufacture pain for profit. I chose not to.

I was grateful I was alive, much less unhurt.

I have never regretted it.

What I didn't realize at the time was that this wouldn't be my last lesson involving attorneys; it was simply the most personal one. Years later, when my world expanded from survival-level sales jobs to managing thousands of employees inside a massive corporation, attorneys would reappear in a very different role. This time it wasn't about whether I would profit from calling myself a victim; it was about what happens when lawyers, policies, and fear collide inside organizations that have lost all common sense.

At MCI Long Distance, I managed over one thousand employees and, as a result, saw more legal nonsense than one person should reasonably be expected to process in a lifetime.

Cases came across my desk that were so absurd you had to blink twice to make sure you were reading them correctly. Let me share one with you that I have shared with others at speaking engagements, a story other consultants have heard and love to retell, though they always get it wrong. They fixate on the bullwhip, but that's not the story at all. The real story is that I didn't recognize, at the time, what an absolute circus I was allowing to unfold. I was greenlighting the kind of foolishness that would someday make me look like the biggest idiot in a courtroom. Looking back, I shouldn't have allowed a bullwhip within ten miles of that sales floor.

Back when our Austin facility started outperforming every center in the country, four sales in four hours compared to everyone else's one, corporate decided to expand us. We were the "golden child" facility. We were high-tech before anyone even knew what that meant. We had PCs when most people still thought "PC" meant "politically correct." Behind a glass partition sat a mainframe the size of a Buick that probably had less power than the phone in your pocket today, but back then it was state-of-the-art.

Our staff were mostly bright part-time college students who loved pounding those function keys to maneuver through a sale. It was fast, it was fun, and the numbers were incredible.

One day, I inherited a brand-new supervisor transferred from New York. He was twenty-three, handsome, energetic, and thrilled to be in Austin. Not long after arriving, he did what any newly transplanted New Yorker considers an obvious rite of passage: He went to Mexico.

He came back with mariachis, bells, a giant sombrero, and a bullwhip.

His job was to walk the aisles and keep his teams motivated. And he did that, spectacularly. The staff adored him. Each day he brought in another piece of Mexican flair. Each lasted a few days. Then came the bullwhip.

He strutted up and down the aisles, cracking it theatrically. The employees were laughing so hard they could barely breathe. Sales numbers soared even higher. Apparently, nothing motivates like the sound of a dramatic crack behind you.

The thrill was short-lived, and everything went back to Ron's apartment.

Three months later, I was in my office early one morning when the HR director called.

"Sharon, have you seen *The Villager* today?"

The Villager was one of Austin's leading newspapers serving the Black community at the time.

"No, why?"

"Sit down. Let me read you the headline."

I sat.

"MCI Employee Beaten with Bullwhip."

For a moment, the words didn't even compute. Then it all rushed back.

Oh. My. Goodness. The bullwhip.

The story claimed that Ron, the supervisor, had beaten an employee across the back. The employee's mother was prepared to testify that she had seen blood rolling down his back. According to the claim, the employee tried to forget the incident, but every time he drove to a job interview, the trauma overwhelmed him halfway there, causing him to "go crazy" and forget where he was going.

Within days, we received the EEOC filing. In the section labeled "Other," someone had handwritten: What is MCI's policy on bullwhips?

Then came the lawsuit, two hundred and fifty pages of fiction that should have won an award.

MCI's attorneys decided to settle for $80,000. This was decades ago, equivalent to roughly $800,000 today. I was furious. I lost all respect for leadership in that moment.

Ironically, when I eventually left the company, they were so terrified I might sue them that they quietly handed me a $20,000 check without me filing a claim.

And that was my introduction to corporate attorneys.

It was only the beginning.

I can still remember exactly where I was when the phone call came in.

I was in the warehouse folding towels (part towels, part Shwipes), doing the kind of work you do yourself when you can't afford not to.

I answered, "Upstairs Maid," and immediately knew this wasn't a friendly call.

They introduced themselves as attorneys for AT&T and said they wanted to meet with me.

AT&T was suing MCI over falsified sales during the long-distance rollover period, when every household in the country suddenly had to choose a carrier. The process had been chaotic, confusing, and ripe for abuse. Telemarketing centers popped up everywhere, and sales were sometimes created more creatively than honestly.

I knew it was going on. Several of us did. That was one of the major reasons I left MCI. One of my comanagers, a man they decided to make my boss, was falsifying sales from the obituaries. I knew that. I think MCI knew I knew that. I believe that's why I received a $20,000 severance check.

Let me be clear: I did not fabricate a single sale. But I wasn't naïve enough to pretend the system around me was clean.

That mattered now. Anything I could tell AT&T would have been secondhand. I had documentation, but no firsthand wrongdoing of my own. I didn't offer that distinction.

I agreed to meet with them.

During one of our conversations, I asked a question I already knew I shouldn't ask unless I was prepared for the answer.

"Do you ever pay anyone for testifying?"

They said yes. That could be arranged.

I didn't sleep much after that.

Money was tight. Very tight. I was folding towels at midnight because I couldn't afford to find staff. A sudden infusion of cash would have helped, more than I wanted to admit.

But my father's voice kept running through my head: "You never get something for nothing."

The next morning, I called MCI and told them AT&T had approached me.

They handled it professionally. They paid for parking, took me to dinner, and listened. They told me I was the cleanest separation they'd ever had and that I could have asked for far more than $20,000 when I left.

The next day, we arrived early at the conference room.

When the AT&T attorneys walked in and saw me seated between the MCI attorneys, they stopped cold.

The deposition was canceled. No testimony. No follow-up.

I don't know what happened to that case. But I do know what happened to me.

That was the first time, as a business owner, I learned how attorneys really make money: not by fixing problems but by finding leverage. By identifying fear. By seeing who is willing to trade discomfort for cash.

I slept better that night than I had in weeks.

And it wouldn't be the last time I'd be asked to decide which side of that line I was willing to stand on.

Once your business crosses the million-dollar mark, you become prey. Before $1M, if a cleaner broke a cup, the client said, "Don't worry about it." After $1M, the same cup became a "family heirloom imported from France in 1496."

Everything escalates. Everyone assumes you have money. Everyone sees you as a payday.

My next encounter came shortly after we crossed that threshold. I hired a cleaner whose husband worked for ArtCarved Rings who had recently transferred him to Austin from New York. She worked for me exactly two weeks before she fell while carrying garbage to a customer's central trash area.

She came into the office and said her knee hurt a bit, but she didn't think she needed a doctor. I was relieved.

The next morning, she called.

"I'm really hurting today. I don't think I can come in."

I asked if she'd seen a doctor. She hadn't yet but planned to. I told her I had a list of doctors suggested. She said she'd find her own.

That should have been my first red flag.

She did not return to work, and I did not hear from her for three weeks when a thick envelope arrived: sixty-two pages of deposition and a demand for $10,000.

I hired an attorney I'd met at a chamber luncheon. He charged $3,000 to attempt an out-of-court settlement. The other side ignored his letters. Their replies were hostile.

Then he discovered something interesting: Her husband was also suing his employer and had just lost his disability income. The company he was suing had uncovered the fraudulence of his claim. Suddenly, this couple had no income at all.

Four days before Christmas, my attorney walked into my office.

"Offer her $3,200."

I asked why.

"They need Christmas money."

She accepted the same day.

It cost me $6,200 in total. A lot, but far less than a trial. Her deposition claimed our cleaners should have had valets to carry trash because "a valet could better identify hazards."

Valets. For trash. We probably would have won, but the cost of winning simply wasn't worth it.

I considered that settlement a blessing. I was done with it, and it cost less than $10,000.

My third lesson in attorneys, and by far the scariest, came years later, after I thought I already understood how these situations worked.

I hired a cleaner who, on paper, was a gift. She could drive, spoke both English and Spanish, and was steady and reliable. After about eight months, she told me her husband would soon be out of jail and asked if I would consider hiring him.

He had been working for a rancher near our property, and we needed work done at our ranch, so I agreed. We hired him as contract labor. His job was clearing cedar. Texas cedar grows thick and low, more like a giant bush than a tree. When you cut the bottoms properly, the land opens up and looks beautiful. It's hard, dirty work.

When he started, he told me very clearly that he wasn't interested in overtime. What he wanted was steady work. Ideally, fifty hours a week.

So we gave him fifty hours a week.

For nearly a year, he worked consistently. He accomplished a tremendous amount of work. He also started one fire that required the fire department, which we handled without drama. Years later, we found beer cans hidden under the trees, but at the time, we didn't know that. We were focused on the work getting done, and it was.

When the ranch project ended, he had no choice but to come into the company if he wanted to keep working. Coincidentally, our window and carpet technician had just left, a story you heard earlier, so we brought him into that role. He moved from contract labor into a salaried position and worked full-time. In hindsight, I'm not sure he ever really wanted that job, but we made room for him anyway.

Then one day, his wife got into an accident in one of our company cars.

It was her fault. But ambulance chasers don't wait for facts.

They contacted her, got an appointment, and once they realized there wasn't much of a case on the accident itself, they pivoted. But not before planting ideas.

Suddenly, we were facing two lawsuits.

One claimed unpaid overtime for every extra hour the husband had worked on our ranch for an entire year, about $10,000.

The second was far more dangerous.

She claimed she should have been paid overtime for all the time she spent picking up her partners in the morning and driving them to the first job.

That was a benefit of our company, not a requirement. We provided company cars to drivers and allowed them to take the cars home at night. In the morning, the driver would pick up their partners on the way to the first job. It was a perk. A recruiting advantage. Not a condition of employment. I also had partners who didn't drive at all.

Her attorneys began talking about a class-action lawsuit.

If they succeeded, we were done.

A quarter of a million dollars. Possibly half a million. We would not survive it.

I called my best friend, who would later become my divorce attorney, and she took me to a very high-powered attorney who taught law at UT. Her rate was $300 an hour. Her assistant's rate was $175, and the assistant attended every meeting.

The first session alone cost $1,500 just to explain the situation.

They dug and dug and didn't like what they were finding. It looked bad. It looked like we might lose. And the invoices kept coming.

I was devastated.

Then one day, I called another close friend, Sharon, who was the HR director at UWM. I explained the entire situation to her, start to finish.

She listened quietly and then asked one simple question: "Was driving a condition of employment?"

No, it wasn't. I had supervisors who drove and supervisors who didn't. Driving was never required.

She said, "Then the driving could be considered voluntary, not unpaid work."

I hung up and immediately called the $300-an-hour attorney.

She paused. Then she said, "That might work."

And it did.

We settled the class-action threat for one dollar.

I still had to pay the husband $10,000 in overtime, and I paid approximately $15,000 in legal fees, but we survived. Barely.

That was the moment I learned, once and for all, that attorneys are like doctors: If you're not thinking for yourself, you're in trouble.

They are there to file papers, argue positions, and bill hours. The thinking, the real thinking, has to come from you.

By then, I thought I had learned every attorney lesson there was to learn.

I was wrong.

By 2006, the country had entered a very different chapter, especially in Texas. Undocumented workers had always been part of the landscape, but quietly, invisibly. That changed. By the mid-2000s, they were prevalent, across service industries nationwide, and suddenly, everyone noticed.

Immigration marches filled the streets. Enforcement grew louder, more aggressive, more public. INS became ICE, and with that name change came fear. Real fear. Not theoretical fear, everyday fear.

We felt it in our industry. We felt it in our offices.

Regina used to joke that if ICE ever showed up, she'd jump into the dumpster behind the office, pull the lid down, and hope they didn't look inside. I always thought it was a clever plan. I was never quite sure how she intended to climb into the garbage can so quickly, but we never got around to a practice run.

We laughed, but the tension was real.

That fear set the stage for my final attorney lesson before my divorce attorneys.

In the spring of 2006, Mike and I planned a long trip, Rome and a cruise. The company was doing $1.7 million. We had stability. But the immigration climate made me uneasy.

I assumed ICE would respond aggressively.

I was about to get on a boat and be unreachable.

So I hired an ICE attorney.

He told me not to worry. He explained how enforcement worked back then. He said raids wouldn't happen in offices like mine. He reassured me.

But to call him if something did happen, I needed a retainer.

Five thousand dollars.

I paid it.

Nothing happened.

Two years later, during my divorce, I asked for the money back.

There was nothing to return.

They had done "research."

That's when I learned something critical.

Sometimes attorneys sell peace of mind, not solutions. Fear is expensive. And once you stop thinking for yourself, you will pay for it.

And when you give an attorney money, you will never get it back.

CHAPTER 16

THE SOFTWARE SAGA

By the time I finished learning what attorneys could cost a business, financially, emotionally, and existentially, I believed I had finally seen every possible way control could slip through my fingers. I was wrong. Because while attorneys exploit fear after something goes wrong, there is another kind of danger that creeps in much earlier, much quieter, and often disguised as growth itself. It doesn't arrive with threats or depositions or envelopes thick with paper. It arrives with success. With more clients than systems. With good intentions and no structure. And that is where the next lesson begins.

There's something almost fable-like about how we tracked our first two hundred repeat clients. Picture it: oversized desktop PCs squatting on our desks like stubborn appliances that could barely type a letter, rudimentary financial software that crashed if you so much as thought about clicking the wrong button, and absolutely zero scheduling software, especially not for a cleaning service. That technology simply didn't exist yet.

When we hit about fifty clients, I started losing control.

At first, I did what every desperate owner does when the business grows faster than the infrastructure: I wrote everything down. Names, addresses, cleaning dates, everything. Paper was my "system." And paper worked…for about six months. Then it didn't. Then it became what paper always becomes when you're scaling: a slow-motion drowning.

So I graduated to Excel, which at the time felt like I had just upgraded into NASA.

I built my own numbering system because I needed something fast and clean. Weekly clients got a one hundred number. Biweekly clients got two hundred. Every three weeks clients got three hundred. Monthly clients got four hundred. When a new client came in, I'd assign them the next available number in their category and drop them into the spreadsheet.

It was the closest thing we had to order.

But Excel didn't solve the schedule; it just organized the chaos.

Because once every five weeks, Mike and I would dedicate two full days to what I can only describe as scheduling hell.

We'd sit at a picnic table on the property we'd just bought, property we were living on in tents because we didn't have the money to hire a builder yet. We had a living room tent, a bedroom tent, and a kitchen tent. They were actually quite cute now that I think about it. And because we were apparently trying to make "poverty camping" feel like hospitality, we even bought a guest tent for the weekend my mother came to stay with us.

But I digress.

Here's how it worked.

Mike would sit across from me holding the old schedule like it was sacred text. I'd have a fresh, blank calendar spread out in front of me, clean, open, and optimistic for about twelve minutes.

He would read out each client number, never the name, because there wasn't enough room on those calendars to write full names.

"Client 142," he'd call out.

I'd flip back to the old calendar. "They were cleaned on the twelfth. Weekly. So they go on the nineteenth, twenty-sixth, and…" I'd count forward and write the number five times across the calendar, like I was doing math homework for a business that refused to behave.

"Client 287."

"Every other week. Last cleaned on the fifteenth. Goes on the twenty-ninth and then the twelfth of next month."

And we'd do it again.

And again.

And again.

Hours. And hours. And hours.

The entire process took a full weekend, sometimes longer if we had grown significantly that month. We weren't "planning." We were manually scheduling every single client for the next five weeks like two exhausted librarians organizing a thousand books while the building is on fire.

Then I would work off those handwritten calendars, booking new clients completely "in the blind."

When a new client called, I'd look backward to see what time slots were still open and just hope they'd still be available when I flipped forward five weeks. Every five weeks, we'd repeat the whole nightmare and then spend the first part of the new schedule correcting whatever disasters I'd created by guessing.

It was insanity.

It took us about three years to reach two hundred repeat clients. And by then, I wasn't just tired; I was in over my head. I could feel control slipping. Not just of the schedule, of the entire business.

And then, like some strange moment of perfect timing, a woman I used to work with at MCI Long Distance called me with news.

Her husband had just lost his job.

"He's high-tech," she said. A programmer. A man who could write MS-DOS.

For anyone who doesn't know what MS-DOS is, let me put it this way: If you do know, you're probably smiling right now. And if you don't know, just trust me, getting MS-DOS to do computations was no small feat.

He came into my office one afternoon and made me an offer.

"I'll write you a program," he said. "Something that schedules clients, tracks their data, the whole thing."

"How much?" I asked, bracing myself.

"Three hundred dollars."

I blinked. "Three hundred? That's it?"

"I just want to learn and teach myself. This'll give me the opportunity."

Now granted, this was 1991. But even then, $300 was ridiculously cheap for custom software. I said yes immediately.

It took him about four weeks.

Then one day he walked into the office, proud as could be, and laid down my schedule. I must admit, it looked beautiful, clean lines, organized columns, everything perfectly aligned. It looked like order.

There was just one problem.

"Every client was listed only once on the calendar. Four times this month. Not once."

His face went pale. "You mean they need to be on here multiple times?"

"Yes," I said. "Weekly clients get cleaned every week. That's… that's four times a month."

I watched the realization hit him like a brick. He picked up the paperwork, turned around, and walked out the door without saying another word.

I genuinely thought I would never see him again.

But I was wrong.

About two weeks later, he walked back in, with corrected software, and it worked beautifully. We used that software all the way up to $1.2 million in revenue.

Then, once again, it started getting out of control.

The biggest issue? The system didn't keep data on canceled clients or one-time clients. So every time somebody called, we'd have to dig through manual files to find their information, so we didn't have to take it all over again. It was laborious. It was time-consuming. It was the kind of thing that doesn't look like a big problem until you're doing it fifty times a week.

So I started software hunting.

Actually, I got telemarketed by someone from California who had software that sounded exactly like what I needed. I was thrilled. I was excited. I was ready to be rescued.

It cost $3,600.

After watching a demo, I bought it.

Nancy was my office manager at the time—sharp, organized, and experienced. She'd worked for a temporary agency franchise before joining us, so she was pretty adept at software. She spent approximately fifty-two hours entering all of our repeat client data into that system: name, address, phone number, cleaning frequency, special instructions, everything.

Fifty-two hours.

We should have been smart enough to test it with two clients first.

We weren't.

After Nancy entered the last client, we gathered around the computer like proud parents watching a child take its first steps. We were ready to schedule our first job.

The client wanted a 7:30 a.m. start time.

I clicked through the screens, selected the client, chose the date, and tried to enter 7:30 a.m.

Nothing.

I tried again.

Still nothing.

So I called the software company.

"Hi, I'm having trouble scheduling a client for seven thirty in the morning. The system won't let me enter that time."

"Oh," the rep said cheerfully, "that's because it doesn't schedule before 8:00 a.m."

I froze. "What do you mean it doesn't schedule before eight o'clock?"

"The system starts at 8:00 a.m. Who would want somebody to come to their house before 8:00 in the morning anyway?"

"We have several clients who meet us at seven thirty before they leave for work."

"Well," the rep said, like this was completely reasonable, "you can't do that anymore. You'll have to tell them it has to be eight o'clock."

I couldn't believe what I was hearing.

They weren't offering a fix. They were telling me to change my business to fit their software.

"No software company," I said slowly, "will ever tell me how to run my customer service or my company."

We never used it again.

One of my several nightmare decisions wasted $3,600. Not as brutal as the $6,600 visa card scam, but not good. And now I was afraid to try any other software.

That experience taught me something important: There simply was no software written yet for residential cleaning services. We were too small. Too niche. Too specific in our needs.

So we stumbled along, hobbled along, on our MS-DOS software for another year and a half. Then one day, a weekly client called to cancel.

He had worked for Michael Dell and had just lost his job. He couldn't afford weekly cleanings anymore.

And I had a thought.

"Why don't we trade services?" I suggested.

"What do you mean?"

I knew he was a programmer.

"How would you like to write a software program for my cleaning service? We'll keep cleaning your house, and you write us exactly what we need."

"Sure," he said. "Why not?"

He came into the office almost immediately. He asked questions. He looked at what we had. He took notes. Then he left.

Two weeks later, he walked back in with the perfect software system.

Perfect.

It did things that software still doesn't do today. He designed it exactly the way I asked. We only ended up cleaning his house two more times because he got another job and was flying off to some foreign country, but the software stayed.

We were still using it when I left the company in 2008.

Good software is absolutely mandatory when running any home service business. Shortly after I left The Upstairs Maid, several software companies began developing systems specifically designed for service businesses. Two of the early platforms that are still thriving today are ZenMaid and Jobber, and I would encourage any owner to take a look at them. That said, there are many other excellent software options available today, and new ones continue to appear as the industry grows.

Modern service software does far more than simply schedule clients. It can quote the job, schedule the appointment, remind the client when their cleaning date is approaching, process payments, deposit funds directly into your bank account, and track every activity in your business in real time. Some platforms will even help with marketing—automatically sending messages to repeat clients and reaching out to customers who have canceled.

It does it all.

And yet I must ask: Why aren't there more $20, $30, $40 million cleaning companies?

People's eyes still pop when they meet someone running a $10 million operation. So what are staff members doing all day these days?

Remember, I didn't have any software until I had two hundred repeat clients.

When clients needed to be moved to a different cleaning date, there was no Internet and no texting. I had to call them on the phone. If they didn't answer, I left a voicemail. Then I called again. And again. Until someone confirmed.

If a team had a skip, a client who wasn't home or canceled at the last minute, I had no way to get ahold of them.

We built a system: I would call the house, let the phone ring twice, hang up, then call back. If they were there, they'd pick up the second time because they'd know it was me. Otherwise, it went to voicemail, and I wasted time waiting.

If a team had four jobs that day, I might go through that routine three out of four times before I could reach them.

Why?

Because I let the teams run their schedules in the way that made the most sense to them and the client. I wish I would have never changed that system, because they certainly knew when the babies were taking their naps better than I did.

It was, of course, Colleen who made me realize this.

I was in my office scheduling one day when Colleen came storming in, half annoyed as usual.

"Why'd you put Mrs. Henderson at two? You know her baby sleeps then."

I looked up. "No, I didn't know her baby sleeps then. How would I know that?"

Colleen planted her hands on her hips. "You should just let me do the scheduling."

Clarity hit me and I said, "That's actually a really good idea."
And so I did.

I gave the team supervisors the schedules for Tuesday, Wednesday, and Thursday, and again for Friday and Monday, the days they came into the office for check-in and check-out. They'd go home that night, call their own clients, and tell them what time they'd be there the next day if the time varied.

That cut way down on my phone calls, and clients were much happier because the cleaners knew their schedules better than I did.

But monthly clients still had to be called by us to verify their cleaning dates. We tracked them manually on a sheet that hung in the middle office, with all the monthly clients for the upcoming week written on it. When someone confirmed, we'd highlight their name. Then we'd call everyone who didn't confirm that night. It was a lot of phone calls.

I fixed these issues as soon as technology allowed.

I got the cleaners pagers as soon as they were available. We upgraded to cell phones as soon as they became accessible, and we paid for them, because back then very few people had cell phones.

Of course, we had a lesson there too.

Several months after we got the cell phones, one of them came in with a bill for over $1,000 because one of the cleaners was calling her boyfriend in jail.

That prompted Mike to find phones we could program to only call the office. I wonder if those are still available today. It might actually be better to give cleaners company phones and not allow them to use their own during the day.

But even with pagers, cleaners often had to find a payphone to call us back.

Every Thursday, the cleaners left with a bag full of quarters for payphones.

And every time it rained, I hated it.

Because I would inevitably lose a driving supervisor, especially if they had a new job scheduled. And this was a time when there was no GPS. Not even TomToms yet. Everything was done with a paper map.

If it was raining and they couldn't read the map or find the client's house, they'd stop at a payphone.

Picture it: They're standing in the rain because they can't find their umbrella, because in Texas, it didn't rain much, so who kept track of umbrellas? They're soaked, frustrated, calling me for directions. I'd give map directions. They'd climb back into the car and drive off to try again.

If you heard from them a second time, it was touch-and-go whether you'd ever see that cleaner again.

Maybe you'd get a second chance, but when they called from that second payphone in the pouring rain, you better be careful not to sound angry, even though you'd just gotten a call from the client who was furious and screaming at you because the team was not there yet.

In that moment, anger better not roll downhill, or you'd find yourself cleaning that house yourself.

I received more than one phone call that began with: "You can pick your car up at the HEB parking lot."

Today's technology makes running a home service business 100 percent easier. Let me give you another example.

There was no credit-card processing for small service businesses in 1988 when we first started. Everyone left a check or cash.

Every check had to be manually entered into our software. Then a tape total had to be run on the adding machine. That tape total had to balance back to the batch on the computer. When we were running two hundred repeat clients and bringing in serious revenue, those tape totals got very large, even when we split them in half. We could spend an embarrassing amount of time trying to find a keypunch error.

Then the checks had to be taken to the bank.

We did this twice a week when the teams came in for check-in and check-out. Keri and Nancy would grab those checks as fast as they could and try to get them all entered by customer before the team left, just in case one was missing.

Many a check was washed in a cleaner's jeans because they forgot to take it out of their pocket when they got home. Then you had to go through the hassle of getting another check from the client, and they usually wanted to stop payment on the first one, which cost $20.

These are all things no one has to deal with today.

We began accepting credit cards as soon as our bank approved it. It was well worth the 3 percent charge.

Technology has revolutionized this industry.

What used to take two full days every five weeks now takes seconds. What used to require bags of quarters and rain-soaked cleaners at payphones now happens with a single text. What used to involve manual check entries and bank runs now processes automatically while you sleep.

And yet I still wonder:

If I built a million-dollar company using paper calendars, MS-DOS software, and a picnic-table scheduling system, what's stopping today's owners, with all this incredible technology, from building $40 million companies?

The tools are there. The software exists. The systems work.

But the real growth engine in this business has never been technology; it's repeat clients.

Repeat clients don't cost you money to advertise again. They don't require a new sales pitch every week. They quietly build your revenue in the background, month after month, year after year, as long as you don't lose them.

So maybe the real issue isn't access to better tools.

Maybe it's whether the fundamentals are being applied consistently, whether the service is repeatable, the systems are repeatable, and the client experience is repeatable.

Because that's what allows a company to grow without constantly starting over.

Even if you're running it all from a tent.

CHAPTER 17

THE DISCIPLINE OF CHOICE

For most of my career, I believed discipline was about action, showing up, working harder, pushing through, doing more.

What I eventually learned is that behavior is the final step in the process, not the first. Long before discipline shows up in action, it shows up in thinking. And if that's true, then leadership isn't a title; it's a decision you make again and again, long before anyone ever sees your actions.

If you don't discipline your thoughts, they will discipline you.

Every business owner hears the same internal dialogue eventually:

This won't work.

This is too hard.

Other people have it easier.

My employees don't care.

The timing isn't right.

Left unchecked, those thoughts become beliefs. And beliefs quietly shape decisions.

The most successful people I've known weren't immune to negative thinking. They were unwilling to let it run the show. They questioned their assumptions. When something went wrong, they didn't immediately assign blame: to themselves, their employees, or circumstances. They asked better questions.

What can I learn from this?

What needs to change?

What part of this is actually within my control?

That discipline matters, especially in leadership.

Leaders don't just manage outcomes; they manage atmosphere. When an owner spirals into fear or frustration, it spreads. When an owner stays grounded and solution focused, that spreads too. Teams take their emotional cues from the top, whether we like it or not.

I've seen owners with strong systems fail because they allowed their thinking to drift into resentment, suspicion, or defeat. I've also seen owners with far fewer resources succeed because they refused to let a setback define the future.

The difference was never intelligence. It wasn't experience. It wasn't opportunity. It was discipline over thinking.

Every challenge presents a choice. You can treat it as confirmation that something is broken beyond repair, or you can treat it as information. One path leads to stagnation. The other leads to progress.

People talk about change as if it happens to them. It doesn't. Change is the result of a decision, or the refusal to make one.

Over the years, I've watched owners complain about the same problems month after month, sometimes year after year. The names change. The faces change. But the problems don't. When that happens, it's rarely because the business is cursed or the industry is impossible. It's almost always because the choices haven't changed.

Everything in a business comes down to choice: You choose whether to implement systems or rely on hope. You choose whether to train or assume. You choose standards, structure, and expectations. And once you make those choices, your employees make theirs.

When performance slips or behavior misses the mark, the issue isn't punishment; it's direction. Consequences, when handled correctly, are not about control. They are tools for correction and growth.

But all of that assumes the right priorities were chosen in the first place.

Sometimes the cost of poor choices isn't obvious immediately.

I once worked in the office of an owner named Barbara. She was desperate for employees. The company was short-staffed, overwhelmed, and scrambling daily.

While Barbara was at a doctor's appointment one afternoon, I sat in her car with a list of previous applicants, people who had interviewed, no-showed, or been passed over. Recruiting should always include a treasure chest. If someone didn't show up, the first question should be why, not next.

One of those no-shows answered the phone. She explained that her child had been in an accident on the day of her interview. In the chaos, she completely forgot to call.

We scheduled another interview. She arrived composed, articulate, professional, and deeply grateful for the second chance. She was clearly overqualified. We hired her on the spot.

What surprised me most during the interview wasn't her resume. It was what she valued about the company.

Two things stood out to her above all else. First, that the company provided three branded T-shirts at no cost. Second, that the company had company vehicles.

Those details mattered to her. They made her feel legitimate. Valued. Part of something professional.

We hired her to start the very next day.

That's when we realized there were no T-shirts. None.

Barbara hadn't ordered them, not because she couldn't afford them and not because of supply issues, but because she couldn't decide what color she wanted next. She kept changing her mind. Her concern about image, about getting the color just right, outweighed the basic reality that employees actually needed uniforms to do their jobs.

Her vanity overruled practicality.

That choice sent a message, whether she intended it or not.

First impressions are lasting impressions. And while the new hire handled it graciously, the disappointment was visible. The company had promised professionalism and failed to deliver on something basic.

We sent her home that night with training materials. She studied them thoroughly—it was obvious the next morning. When we went into the field, she worked hard, paid attention, and pushed herself.

She wasn't used to dirt.

I remember one moment clearly. We were in a repeat client's home, and she opened a shower caddy filled with old soap, shampoo residue, and grime. It was disgusting. She looked at me like I had lost my mind.

"You want me to clean that?" her eyes said.

We worked through it.

By the time I left that office, she was a fast, capable, confident cleaner— exactly the kind of employee companies say they're looking for.

About three weeks later, I called Barbara to check in.

"She's not with us anymore," Barbara said, laughing.

I was stunned. I asked what happened.

She explained that the employee had a serious fear of snakes and had been very clear about it during training. She said she would clean anything, anywhere as long as she was never sent to a house with a snake.

A week after I left, she was scheduled at a home with a large snake in a glass enclosure. While dusting a bedroom, she heard movement, saw the enclosure, panicked, and ran. She grabbed the company car and left her teammate behind.

Barbara was still laughing as she told me the story.

I wasn't.

What disturbed me wasn't the fear of snakes; it was the complete disregard for the employee and the casual way the situation was dismissed. How could someone schedule her for that house knowing what they knew? And how could an owner find humor in a situation that put one employee in danger and abandoned another?

That moment told me everything I needed to know.

This wasn't a one-off mistake. It was a reflection of priorities.

I learned long ago that there are three priorities in a company and the order matters.

First, the company.

Second, the employees.

Third, yourself.

Barbara had it backward.

She put herself first, her preferences, her convenience, her image. The company came second. And the employees came last.

That isn't leadership.

That's ego.

And ego always costs more than it's worth.

Leadership lives in priorities. And priorities are revealed not in what we say, but in the smallest choices we make, especially when no one is watching.

Choice comes first. Change follows. And champions are made, or lost, in the space between the two.

And once you choose differently, you lead differently, and that is how you put hope where others think there is none.

CHAPTER 18

PUTTING HOPE WHERE OTHERS THINK THERE IS NONE

Hope is the universal emotion that will drive anyone to do anything.

I didn't learn that from a leadership seminar, and I didn't learn it from a book. I learned it the way most owners learn everything, by standing in the middle of a problem with no manual, no safety net, and no time to be delicate.

When Mike and I took over The Upstairs Maid, there were days when the business felt like a living thing that needed to be fed hourly. The mortgage didn't care if I had a rough week. The phone didn't stop ringing because I was tired. And the truth was, our company didn't have the luxury of easing into anything.

We weren't just building a business. We were building a future—fast, without the Internet, without templates, and without anyone to tell us what to do next.

In those early months, every hire mattered. Not because I was trying to grow an empire, but because I was trying to keep the doors open.

What I didn't expect was this: The people who came through our door weren't just looking for a job. They were looking for hope.

I could see it before they ever opened their mouths. Most applicants didn't walk in with confidence. They walked in with caution, like they didn't want to take up too much space. Some were polite and quiet. Some were overly talkative because nervous people can't tolerate silence. Some came in with smiles that looked practiced, like something they wore to survive hard seasons.

And almost every one of them carried the same unspoken question: Is this going to be another place where I fail?

Owners like to talk about hiring good people, like the right employee walks in fully formed, clean history, strong work ethic, perfect attitude, and an inner drive that needs no coaching.

That is not real life.

Real life is people who have been bruised by life but showing up anyway.

Some had been fired. Some had quit before being fired. Some had bounced from job to job, not because they were lazy but because nobody ever trained them properly. Some had been treated like they were disposable. Some had been told, directly or indirectly, that they weren't smart enough to do anything better.

You can say you're hiring for a cleaning company, but what you're really doing is interviewing someone's belief system. And most belief systems walking through the door are running low.

That's why hope matters. Hope is not a warm feeling. Hope is fuel.

Hope is what gets someone to wake up and try again after life has taught them to expect disappointment.

But here's the thing: Most people don't need a pep talk. They don't need you to "pump them up." They need something far more practical than that.

They need a path.

They need to know what winning looks like.

They need to know what to do first.

That sounds simple, but it's rare. Most people are hired and then tossed into confusion with a smile and the words, "You'll catch on."

"You'll catch on" is not training. "You'll catch on" is a slow-motion quitting notice.

Because when people don't know what to do, they make mistakes. When they make mistakes, they feel embarrassed. When they feel embarrassed, they hide or shoot the messenger. Either way, they get criticized. And when they get criticized without a clear way forward, they leave.

Not always with a goodbye. Sometimes they just don't show up.

I learned that lesson long before I ever owned a cleaning company.

When I worked at MCI, I was standing in a hallway one day with a few other managers. We were laughing, really laughing, about an employee we considered a nerd. This was back when nerds weren't cool. In our minds, this person thought they knew everything. They were bold, brassy, a little too confident for our taste.

And then we caught them in a mistake. We gave them a written warning.

The next day, they didn't show up. No call. No explanation. Nothing.

We laughed even harder. Where's their pride now?

Then our manager, Craig, walked up and asked what we were talking about. When we told him, still half smiling, his face changed instantly.

"That's the most disgusting thing I've ever heard," he said.

We stopped laughing.

"The worst reflection on a manager is not an employee quitting," he continued. "It's an employee walking off the job and not even telling you why."

That landed like a punch to the chest.

He said, "When someone disappears like that, it means one of three things: They didn't respect you, they didn't trust you, or they didn't feel safe enough to be honest. And whichever one it is, the failure belongs to leadership, and that is you three."

That moment rewired something in me.

Because it took my attention off the employee and put it back where it belonged: on the environment that leaders create.

Years later, I saw the opposite of that failure when Regina walked into our office.

Regina couldn't speak a word of English. Not one. She and her husband had only been in the States for about six months, and it took us a while to decipher what she was trying to tell us.

What we eventually understood was simple: She needed a job, and she was willing to do anything.

At first, that was all there was to it.

But as we worked with Regina day after day, something else became clear. When we communicated the only way we could—gestures, broken words, laughter, patience—we began to understand her view of the future.

Regina believed she would always be poor. She believed her life's path was already set. Her plan, as she saw it, was to have a dozen children, struggle forever, and eventually return to Mexico with those children.

That was her version of hope.

It wasn't ambitious. It wasn't expansive. But it was the only future she could imagine, because it was the only future she had ever been shown.

Because Regina worked in the office, we were with her every day. She was immersed not just in English, but in our culture, our conversations, our expectations, and our way of thinking.

We laughed together. We explained things. We modeled what "normal" looked like in our world.

Not that there was anything wrong with raising a big family, if that's what someone truly wants. But over time, we realized that wasn't really Regina's dream.

It was simply the only option she'd ever been handed.

As her English improved and she grew more confident, she began to enjoy her job. She took pride in it. She liked being in the office.

And then something shifted.

Within six months, Regina made a decision that changed the course of her family forever. She obtained birth control (brought up from Mexico) and never had another child. Eventually, she became fluent in English. She began volunteering at her son's school. That changed his progress and his confidence. Years later, her daughter became a doctor.

Regina didn't find hope because someone gave her a speech.

She found it because she was placed in an environment where she could see options she had never been shown before.

Hope came quietly, through daily conversations, shared laughter, clear expectations, and the simple belief that her life did not have to follow a single, predetermined script.

And that's when I finally understood something I wish every business owner understood:

Hope is not a mood. Hope is a method.

Hope doesn't arrive as comfort. It arrives as structure.

People think "structure" is cold. They think systems are rigid. They think a step-by-step procedure is controlling.

But I've watched what happens to someone who has been failing for years when you hand them a path that actually works:

Their shoulders relax.

Their face changes.

Their confidence starts to show up again.

Because clarity is hope. Consistency is hope. Knowing what comes next is hope.

When you hand someone a process and say, "Do it in this order," you aren't just telling them how to clean a bathroom; you are telling them, "You can succeed here."

When you train them properly instead of rushing them into a home and hoping they "pick it up," you aren't being picky; you are being merciful.

When you coach them through mistakes without humiliating them, and you hold them accountable without crushing them, you aren't being soft; you are building the kind of stability that hope requires.

People don't rise to the level of your expectations. They rise to the level of your clarity.

The owners who complain the most about "people these days" are usually the ones who offer the least direction. They hire someone, give vague instructions, and then act surprised when results are inconsistent.

But employees don't fail because they're bad. Many fail because the path is unclear.

Confusion creates panic. Panic creates rushing. Rushing creates missed steps. Missed steps create criticism. And criticism without a clear fix creates quitting.

So when I say it's your job, as an owner or manager, to put hope where others think there is none, I'm not talking about being delicate. I'm talking about being strategic.

Hope is not fluff. Hope is a strategy.

And the leaders who do it well aren't the ones who talk the most. They're the ones who learn how to see clearly before they act.

CHAPTER 19

LEADERSHIP VS. MANAGEMENT: WHERE LEADERSHIP ACTUALLY HAPPENS

For a long time, leadership and management were spoken about as if they were the same thing. They are not. They overlap, but they serve different purposes, and when owners confuse them, both suffer.

Management lives in systems. Leadership lives in people.

Management creates order. It answers questions like what gets done, how it gets done, and when. When management is strong, chaos recedes. Quality becomes repeatable. Results become predictable. A well-managed company can function even when the owner is not physically present.

Leadership answers a different set of questions entirely. Why does this matter? Where are we going? Who do you believe I can become? Leadership is not about enforcing behavior; it is about influencing thinking. And thinking is what shapes belief. Belief is what drives action.

That distinction matters more than most owners realize.

I have seen companies with tremendous heart and no structure collapse under their own good intentions. Everyone felt inspired, but nothing worked consistently. I have also seen companies with immaculate systems and no leadership limp along with constant turnover, where everything ran "by the book" and no one cared enough to stay.

The healthiest companies manage the work and lead the people. They do not ask leadership to fix operational chaos, and they do not ask management to create belief.

Understanding where leadership actually happens is the turning point.

Leadership does happen in meetings. But not all leadership happens there.

Meetings are where alignment happens. Meetings are where energy is set, direction is clarified, and belief is seeded. Meetings are where people feel part of something larger than themselves. That "rah-rah" side of leadership matters. It creates momentum. It creates shared language. It creates emotional buy-in.

But meetings are not where lives change.

The real movement of leadership—the kind that changes how people think, what they believe, and ultimately how they act—happens one person at a time.

That is where one-on-ones come in.

There is a principle I learned years ago that has never failed me, and it echoes something Alcoholics Anonymous has understood for decades: Whenever there are two or more people in the room, you have a meeting. The moment a conversation stops being private between two people, it becomes a meeting. And because it is a meeting, it should always remain positive.

Meetings are not the place to contradict people. They are not the place to surface resistance. They are not the place to address what is broken. The moment you introduce negativity in a group setting, you create sides. You create defensiveness. You create a one-versus-many dynamic that no leader ever wins.

I learned that lesson the hard way.

When I was at MCI Long Distance, we were managing a large sales floor. When I arrived, the average salesperson was making one to two sales in a four-hour shift. Over time, through coaching and focus, we got that number up to three. I knew, absolutely knew, we could get it to four.

From a management standpoint, it made sense. The math worked. The opportunity was there. So we made the decision to raise the quota.

Looking back, the mistake wasn't the decision. The mistake was how it was rolled out.

I was still fairly new to management, and I assumed that if something made logical sense, people would eventually come around. I also assumed that if people were upset, the best thing to do was bring them together, explain the reasoning, and answer their questions.

So I scheduled a meeting.

Before it happened, my boss, Craig, asked me if I was sure that was what I wanted to do.

I said, "Yes, absolutely." I wanted to be transparent. I wanted buy-in. I wanted to do the right thing.

He paused and said, "You might want to think about that twice. But let me know how it goes."

I didn't understand what he meant.

I found out quickly.

That meeting was brutal.

The moment I opened the floor, the emotions poured out. People weren't listening to logic. They were reacting to fear. To pressure. To the feeling that something was being taken from them.

One person stood up and said, "You don't care about us. All you care about are numbers."

The room erupted in agreement.

I was one person standing in front of dozens who now felt unified against me. It didn't matter what I said next. The bandwagon had formed, and I was alone on the other side of it. I remember walking out of that meeting with tears in my eyes, stunned by how fast it had gone wrong.

Craig had known exactly what would happen.

What I learned that day stayed with me for the rest of my career: Meetings are not the place to process resistance. They are not the place to change belief. When people are afraid, confused, or threatened, a public setting amplifies emotion and shuts down reason.

Changing behavior requires changing belief. And belief does not change in public.

Belief is formed through thought. Thought comes first. The brain processes information, assigns meaning, and only then forms belief. Action follows belief. Management tries to change action first. Leadership changes thought to belief, and then action can follow naturally.

That kind of work requires privacy.

That is why one-on-ones matter.

One-on-ones are not a "soft" leadership practice. They are where leadership becomes personal. They are where people feel safe enough to admit confusion, fear, resistance, or doubt. They are where you can hear what someone is actually thinking before that thinking hardens into belief.

Once you start doing one-on-ones regularly, you learn something powerful. You can tell what is going on with someone the second they sit down. You can see it in their posture, their eyes, their tone, before they ever say a word. Defeat looks different than defensiveness. Embarrassment feels different than resistance.

Those signals are invisible in meetings.

Meetings hide truth. One-on-ones reveal it.

This is also where leadership shifts from management correction to leadership diagnosis.

Management says, "Here's the rule. Follow it."

Leadership asks, "Help me understand what's happening."

You cannot fix a problem you do not understand. And you cannot truly understand it when you're diagnosing it in a room full of people.

When issues are addressed publicly, people protect themselves. They give surface answers. They say what sounds right. They defend their pride. But in a private conversation, something different happens. Thinking surfaces. And when thinking surfaces, real leadership can begin.

This is where the principle "Seek first to understand before being understood" becomes more than a nice phrase. It becomes a leadership tool.

Understanding changes how you lead. And how you lead determines whether behavior actually changes or just temporarily complies.

I saw this play out countless times in the cleaning industry.

Take long dusting, for example. We would occasionally see complaints come in about high dusting being missed. The management impulse would be to call a meeting and remind everyone to "make sure you're doing long dusting."

That never fixed the problem.

Because the problem wasn't the same for everyone.

In one-on-ones, the truth came out.

One person had lost their long duster and was embarrassed to admit it. Another needed new glasses and genuinely couldn't see what they were missing. Another was rushing because they were afraid of being late to their next job. And occasionally, someone simply didn't care.

Those are four entirely different situations.

One needs equipment. One needs support. One needs scheduling help. One needs accountability.

No meeting in the world would have revealed that. And no blanket reminder would have solved it.

That is the difference between managing behavior and leading people.

Management corrects the symptom. Leadership diagnoses the cause.

And diagnosis only happens in conversations where people feel safe enough to tell the truth.

This is also where leaders must be very clear about the difference between empathy and sympathy.

Empathy is understanding someone's perspective so you can lead correctly.

Sympathy, when misplaced, becomes indulgence; and indulgence is dangerous.

One of the fastest ways to destroy a company from the inside is gossip.

It doesn't announce itself loudly. It usually walks into a one-on-one quietly, disguised as concern or frustration. And if you're not careful, you become the container for it.

If a cleaner came in and started complaining about what someone else was doing, my response was immediate and calm.

"Thank you for sharing that with me," I'd say. "We'll need to let them know."

Almost without fail, the response was panic.

"No, no, no. Don't tell them. They'll be mad at me."

That's when the conversation changed.

"If I can't tell them about it, I can't fix it. And if you didn't bring this to me so it could be fixed, then why did you bring it to me?"

And then I would stop talking.

If they wanted to bring the other employee in and resolve the issue, we'd continue. If not, the conversation ended. Because at that point, the message was clear: This wasn't about solutions. It was about gossip.

And gossip has no place in leadership conversations.

I'd ask one more question, always the same one: "How do you want me to fix this?"

They never had an answer.

That's leadership in one-on-ones. Boundaries matter. Empathy does not mean absorbing dysfunction.

I carried the lesson from MCI into my consulting years. When I rolled out changes, especially changes that affected how cleaners worked, like introducing aprons into companies that had never used them before, I paid close attention to the emotional temperature of the room.

If a team was excited and curious, we made it a celebration. Big rollout. Energy. Momentum.

But most of the time, people weren't excited. They were wary. Change felt like criticism. So we didn't force it publicly. We started quietly. One team, one conversation at a time. We explained the why in one-on-ones. We addressed beliefs before we addressed behavior.

Because you cannot change someone's actions until you change how they think about what they're doing.

That lesson applies everywhere, from cleaning companies to corporate sales floors.

Meetings are where you cast vision and reinforce direction. One-on-ones are where you change lives.

Leadership does not live in binders. It does not live in policies. It does not live in public confrontation.

Leadership lives in people.

And it does its most important work in private conversations, where belief can change, truth can surface, and real growth can begin.

CHAPTER 20

ANCHORED IN THE WRONG PORT

One thing I hadn't talked about yet in this book, and it may be one of the most important decisions you will ever make as a self-employed business owner, is whether to have a partner and who that partner should be.

In fact, I would say choosing the right business partner is probably the second most important decision you will make.

The first is choosing your spouse.

That could be a whole different book, so I won't go deep into it here. But your spouse is your life partner, your emotional foundation, and the person who either steadies you or shakes the ground beneath you. If that relationship isn't healthy, focused, and supportive, it's very difficult for anything else, including a business, to stay strong.

Now, if you happen to choose the right spouse, they might become your business partner. And in theory, there could be no better partner than someone who already shares your life, your trust, and your long-term commitment.

But here's the truth people don't talk about: A perfect spouse does not automatically make a perfect business partner.

Marriage and business require overlapping strengths, but they are not the same job. A great spouse does not have to match your pace, your risk tolerance, your leadership style, or your business energy level. Those differences can make a marriage richer. If your spouse is not your business partner, their role is much simpler and just as important. They don't have to run operations, make decisions, or share your entrepreneurial drive. They only need to do two things: listen and support. That emotional steadiness is often what allows an entrepreneur to carry the weight of building something difficult.

But in business, misaligned energy, urgency, or values can slow growth, stall decisions, and create constant friction.

I didn't fully understand the toll that kind of mismatch takes until years later when a psychologist named Vicki explained it to me in a way I never forgot. She told me I had grown, and the company had grown, to a place where Mike was no longer comfortable. She said he was like a fish out of water. Meanwhile, I kept climbing, stretching, and pushing for more. And every time I wanted to grow, she said, I was picking up that fish and carrying him up the mountain with me.

"Mike's a pretty big fish," she said gently. "Eventually, that's going to wear you out. The kind thing to do might be to put the fish back in the water."

That image hit me hard. I realized I couldn't keep doing what I was doing. I wasn't just building a business. I was carrying an anchor.

So whether your partner is a spouse, a friend, an investor, or someone you just met with a shared idea, they must share more than ownership. They must share values, work ethic, urgency, and, most of all, energy level. They must also have the time to truly be a partner.

A business cannot be someone's side interest if it is someone else's life's work.

I learned this the hard way.

Mike bought the business before I joined him. He paid $30,000 for it. A year later, I came in, what he later jokingly called "the hostile takeover." We had a mortgage based on my corporate salary, and the company consisted of five part-time cleaners working a few days a week. The rest of the time they sat by the pool I had paid for with my MCI earnings.

I saw opportunity. I saw systems that could be built. I saw a future.

Mike saw survival.

Shortly after he bought the business, we went to my boss Craig's house at MCI for a gathering. Craig congratulated Mike and said, "The one thing I learned from Sharon is if it's a good decision, why wait? Implement it fast."

That was how I operated. If something made sense, we moved.

Mike moved differently.

From the beginning, our energy levels didn't match. I was forward-looking, fast-moving, always asking, "How do we make this better?" Mike was cautious, hesitant, often overwhelmed by decisions. Even small operational changes could take months.

My mother once gave us advice based on her years running a farm with my dad. She said the key to working together was simple: Each person needs a clear role, complete trust in the other, and no telling the other how to do their job.

That advice is excellent, if both people actually do their job.

Mike handled bookkeeping and payroll. But things would be left undone. One month our income jumped by $30,000 over average. That was huge for us at the time. When I checked the books, I found he had entered a $3,000 deposit as $30,000.

Trust is impossible without follow-through.

Eventually, he grew tired of being checked, and I grew tired of carrying it all.

Mindset was another divide. Mike saw the glass as half empty. I saw it as half full. I believed in investing in people and thanking them for their work. He rarely did. Employees feel that difference.

This chapter isn't about blaming a spouse. It's about illustrating how deeply a partnership dynamic affects a company.

One bright spot during those years was a fundraiser we hosted for Cleaning for a Reason. A volunteer group ran an old steam train through the Texas Hill Country, and we organized a full-day event. We raised $5,000 that day.

I believed Mike would love the event. Instead, he resisted it.

That's when I understood: When your partner doesn't share your vision, even your biggest wins can feel lonely.

And anything anchored was never my style.

If you remember, I had already worked seventeen jobs in twelve years. That wasn't instability; that was my growth detector. When I felt anchored in growth or income, I moved.

But this time I wasn't just changing jobs. I was changing my life.

At that Christmas train party, I began to sense my husband might be involved with someone in the company. If you remember the "Five Stages Employees Go Through," especially "Stage Three: Intimacy," you might see the irony. The full story belongs in another book called *The Intimate Maid*, so I'll spare you the details.

My instincts were correct.

That didn't create the problems, but it removed the doubt.

So I made a decision that surprised people: I gave him the business.

And I kept the land.

Only four years later, Mike sold the business for a fraction of what we'd been offered only one year prior. The land has multiplied in value thirty-five times.

I don't share that to boast. I share it because sometimes walking away from what you built is walking toward what you were meant to build next.

At a conference years later, I told this story. When I finished, the facilitator asked the audience, "What's the takeaway?"

Someone shouted, "In a divorce, take the land."

We all laughed.

But beneath the humor was truth.

Letting go of that partnership didn't end my story. It cleared the path for the work I was truly meant to do, turning hard-earned lessons into systems, training, and guidance that could help other people grow faster and with less pain than I did.

Everything I've shared in this book grew out of those lessons.

And that's exactly where we're headed next, not just what happened to me—but what all of this can teach you.

CHAPTER 21

WHERE THE REAL LESSONS LIVE

If you've made it this far, you've walked with me through nearly two decades of building The Upstairs Maid, from the early days when I chose to write an employee handbook instead of cleaning houses to the difficult moment when I stepped away from a partnership that had run its course.

This chapter isn't about what happened next. It's about what mattered most.

Because you can read a thousand business books, attend a hundred seminars, and collect advice from every expert you meet. But until you live it, until you face the late-night phone calls, the employee who quits on a Saturday morning, the client who cancels after five years, or the partner who sees the world completely differently than you do, you don't really understand what works.

What I've learned, I learned the hard way.

And if my experience saves you even one major mistake, one sleepless night, or one costly decision, then every story in this book was worth telling.

When I look back over everything we built, everything that worked and everything that didn't, one theme rises above the rest.

Success didn't come from big moments. It came from repeated ones.

Early on, I never focused on revenue. I started with tracking repeat clients. That simple differential changed everything. Revenue feels exciting, but it can fool you. One-time jobs create activity. Repeat clients create stability. And stability is what gives you the breathing room to grow without constantly scrambling for the next sale. That wallpaper chart on the wall wasn't fancy, but it told the truth every single day. It kept us focused on building something that would last.

I also learned that most business owners are sitting on gold and don't even know it. Past clients, canceled accounts, one-time customers—those names are opportunities already earned. I doubled our income by going back to people who had already trusted us once. Meanwhile, I've seen companies spend thousands chasing strangers while ignoring the people who already knew their name. Sometimes growth isn't about going forward. It's about going back and doing a better job the second time.

Community involvement taught me something similar. People call it networking, but to me it was simply showing up, again and again, until our name became familiar. I didn't attend one meeting. I attended dozens. I didn't introduce myself once. I did it hundreds of times, in different rooms, to different people. Over time, our company stopped being "a cleaning service" and became "the cleaning service." That didn't happen from a single conversation. It happened from consistent presence.

Relationships work the same way. Business is built on trust, and trust is built over time. One conversation won't change your life, but a pattern of being helpful, reliable, and honest just might. Many of our biggest opportunities came not from advertising, but from relationships that had been quietly growing for years.

That's also why free exposure often beat paid advertising. When I was invited to speak, to teach, or to share what we were doing, it positioned us as experts in a way no ad ever could. Those opportunities came because I was visible and involved long before anyone handed me a microphone. You can't wait to be discovered. You have to keep showing up until people can't miss you.

None of this was glamorous. Stability rarely is. Growth often looks like doing the same right things repeatedly, even when you're tired of them. One repeat client at a time. One good hire at a time. One improved process at a time. That steady, sometimes boring, consistency is what allows a business to survive long enough to thrive.

And you can't do it alone. A service business grows through people. We offered more than a paycheck; we offered consistency, structure, and respect. We worked to create an environment where people knew what was expected and felt valued for meeting those expectations. Recruiting was hard. Retention was harder. But when people feel seen and supported, they're far more likely to stay and grow with you.

I also learned that success hides in small details. Businesses rarely fail because of one giant mistake. They failed because of a thousand little things no one fixed. The missed follow-up call. The small oversight in a home. The assumption that "It's probably fine." Details, repeated correctly, build trust. Details ignored, repeated often enough, destroy it.

Training was one of the clearest examples of this. Poor training doesn't just cost time; it costs clients, morale, and reputation. Training isn't an expense, it's an investment that pays you back every single day in fewer problems and more confidence from both employees and customers. We made one rule that saved us countless headaches: No one cleaned a client's home until they had been trained and proven ready. That one decision prevented more issues than any policy I ever wrote.

Of course, no matter how well you plan, things will go wrong. Employees quit. Clients cancel. Mistakes happen. The question isn't whether problems will come; the question is whether you've built systems strong enough to handle them when they do. Backup plans, cross-training, and clear procedures turn emergencies into inconveniences instead of disasters.

People themselves taught me another lesson. Not every good worker makes a good team member. Some people thrive alone. Some shine in partnerships. Some simply shouldn't be paired together. As an owner, your job isn't just hiring talent; it's building combinations of people who actually work well together. That takes observation, adjustment, and sometimes tough decisions.

Along the way, I also learned to protect myself. Not everyone in business operates with integrity. There are scams, bad deals, and professionals who don't have your best interests at heart. I learned to trust my instincts, to verify before committing, and to choose advisors carefully. The wrong help can cost more than no help at all.

Technology brought its own lessons. Software can be a powerful tool, but it isn't a magic solution. The right system supports good processes; it doesn't replace them. Chasing trends without understanding your own needs just creates more complexity.

Through all of this, discipline became a daily choice. Not a personality trait, not a burst of motivation, a decision made over and over. Show up. Make the call. Fix the problem. Improve the process. Those small decisions, repeated, compound into results you never could have created with one grand gesture.

Some of the most meaningful results came from believing in people others had overlooked. Some of our best employees were the ones no one else thought would succeed. With training, structure, and consistent support, they grew into incredible team members. Potential reveals itself when someone is given a real chance and steady guidance.

Leadership itself turned out to be more personal than I expected. It doesn't happen in big speeches. It happens in quiet, one-on-one conversations where people feel heard. Management corrects behavior. Leadership changes belief. And belief is what drives consistent action.

The hardest lesson of all came from partnership. A perfect spouse doesn't automatically make a perfect business partner. Business requires shared energy, shared urgency, and shared vision. When those don't match, even success can feel lonely. Letting go of a partnership that isn't working is painful, but sometimes it's the only way forward. Walking away from what we built together opened the door to what I was meant to build next.

When I look back at all nineteen chapters, I don't see isolated stories; I see patterns. Patterns of showing up. Patterns of improving. Patterns of learning, adjusting, and continuing.

Success in a service business isn't complicated. But it is hard.

It requires discipline you must choose daily, systems you must improve repeatedly, people you must support consistently, relationships you must build patiently, and the willingness to keep going when things don't work out the way you planned.

The businesses that succeed aren't the ones with the flashiest ideas. They're the ones that execute consistently, adjust quickly, and refuse to quit.

They are repeatable.

That's why I chose that word for the title of this book. Because success isn't built on one-time effort. It's built on patterns, patterns of action, patterns of improvement, patterns of showing up again and again until the results compound.

You don't have to be perfect. You just have to keep doing the right things long enough for them to work.

Because that's where the real lessons live, not in the big wins, not in the plans, not in the goals written on paper. They live in the daily decisions; the repeated actions; the moments when you choose to show up, improve a process, make the call, fix the mistake, and try again.

That's where your business will be built.

And if you keep showing up there, repeatedly, the results will follow.

FINAL WORDS

If this book has done its job, you won't walk away thinking about my story.

You'll walk away thinking about your own.

About the systems you could tighten. The people you could invest in. The clients you could serve more consistently. The habits you could repeat until they start working for you instead of against you.

Big success rarely comes from big moves. It comes from small right things, done so often they become part of who you are and how your business runs.

So start where you are.

Pick one thing you know you should be doing better. Do it. Then do it again tomorrow.

If you're not sure where to begin, start with the foundation, your training. A well-trained team is one of the most repeatable advantages you can build. If you'd like help creating consistent results through structured training, you can learn more at www. cleansmartacademy.com.

That's how momentum begins. That's how trust is built. That's how businesses grow.

And that's how ordinary effort becomes something extraordinary, not once but over and over again.

www.ingramcontent.com/pod-product-compliance
Lightning Source LLC
Chambersburg PA
CBHW031300160726
47993CB00001B/239